the Unknown Chef

the Unknown Chef

VOLUME II
THE JOURNEY BEGINS
CHEF DAVID CARTER

the Unknown Chef Volume II
The Journey Begins

Copyright ©2018 by David Carter
All rights reserved.

Published by Next Century Publishing
Austin, TX
www.NextCenturyPublishing.com

No part of this publication may be reproduced, stored in a retrieval system, or transmitted in any form or by any means—electronic, mechanical, photocopy, recording, or any other—without the prior permission of the author.

ISBN: 978-1-68102-987-0

Printed in the United States of America

the Unknown Chef

Table Of Contents

INTRODUCTION   1

PERSONAL NOTES   2

SECTION: PURE IMAGINATION   3

PHOTOS   8

ACCOMPLISHMENTS   14

SECTION: GLUTEN   19

SECTION: SEAFOOD   21

SECTION: POULTRY   22

SECTION: PORK/VEAL   23

SECTION: BEEF/DUCK   24

SECTION: VEGETABLES/SALADS   25

SECTION: SWEETS   26

SECTION: BREAKFAST/LUNCH   27

SECTION: SAUCES   28

INDEX   29

RECIPES   34

Pride

Doing what you like to do and wanting to be the best at it. Always learning, seeking, exploring, trying new things to see if they just might work. Letting God be your complete guide and master. In this way, you will want to do what God has meant for you. Be good at it. Thanking him every day for the opportunity to be alive.

Thank you, God, for today.

David W. Carter

Personal Notes:

As I wake every day, my blessing is to God who created everything. Looking out the window, the sky is beautiful and the sun brightens my day. Never stopped to think how life would be without those things being present.

The sun always warms you even when you cannot see it. When you look at the sky it is clear, cloudy or bright. These remind me to always thank God for allowing me to wake this day.

My family, children and friends are blessed as well. The sun and sky help start each day.

Special thanks to:

Chef Richard Davidson Sr.

Shella Hart

Your insights and suggestions were greatly appreciated.

"Pure Imagination" = The Art Of Garde Manger'

The following pictures are a small collection of carvings, plate designs, displays that I have collected over the years. People like to see creative ideas for presenting foods and plate designs. The Ice Carvings were created by a very talented artist, named JOSE'. I had a few pieces but not like his.

"THE TOPIARY TREE"

Pure Imagination:

Place skewer at an angle

Into the pineapple

* Build a Stand

1. Wooden base

2. Hollow pipe

3. Put pipe on base stand

Make sure it's secure.

4. Sturdy enough to hold

At least three pineapples

*Instructions:

1. Cut top and bottom of Pineapple

2. Make a hole in the middle and put in pineapple, stacking ea.

1.   Place leatherleaf in between skewers to hide the pineapple

 Make 3 to 4 cuts on strawberry to create flower and place on skewers. Put green only from onion onto skewers first. Place Baby's Breath wherever you would like to an accent.

Note: let your imagination be free

2.   When assembling tree, the top can be tricky. If the pineapple does not have a top, you can still make one with the tops you cut earlier. Use toothpicks to attach.

PARTS:

Wooden Skewers

Strawberries

Green onions (save white tops for flowers later)

Leatherleaf

Baby's Breath

Pineapple (at least 3)

Paring knife

Chef knife

Scissors

MELON CARVING

1. Draw or trace the picture you want to carve on paper first.
2. Using a pencil, trace from paper onto melon.
3. Cut away gently pieces that are not in the picture.
4. Make sure you cut a flat bottom, for it to stand
5. Take your time.
6. Any variations are a part of your imagination

GREEN ONION FLOWERS

1. Cut white part leaving about 2 inch of green
2. Cut small root off white
3. Lay on cutting board and make small slits in the white part only
4. Place bulb in ice water to allow it to blossom or bloom
5. Use the onion flower as garnish or decorations in carvings, on the tree or plate designs.

Note: you can tie the green parts of several onions to make a small snowball effect.

LOBSTER TAIL

Melt butter in a sauce pan and reserve

Using scissors cut shell down the middle almost to the tail.

Gently spread shell and pull lobster meat up on top of shell.

Flatten tail end to help stand and brush lightly with melted butter, and place under broiler until shell starts to turn pink or orange. Lobster meat should be firm but not hard.

Note: Serve with warm butter on the side (be careful not to overcook)

The Chef's Table

As an upcoming Chef, I had the opportunity to work at the Adams Mark Hotel. During this era, they had a bakery, butcher shop, Gourmet restaurant (The Marker) and a highly-regarded Chef, Mr. Antonio Pologruto. I was asked to participate in his first Chef's Table. This concept is held in the kitchen with a complete banquet set-up. Approximately 8 people including the Chef attended.

I had to create a menu for this occasion. This menu included 5 courses. The two menus that follow where used and created by me. I prepared all the items and sauces.

The review was fantastic.

The Unknown Chef

adam's mark
indianapolis

Chef's Table

February 17, 1989

Appetizer
Medallion of Lobster and Shrimp with Lemon Dill Cream

Salad
Sugar Snappeas, Cauliflower and Red Oakleaf
with Walnut Oil Vinaigrette

Intermezzo

Passion Fruit Granite

Entree
Roast Lamb Loin in Savoy Cabbage with Chive Sauce

Vegetable Ravioli

Fried Polenta with Tomato Chutney

Dessert
Banana Souffle with Pineapple and Sauterne Sauce

adam's mark
indianapolis

Chef's Table
September 15, 1989

Appetizer
Gratin of Zucchini and Basil

Salad
Bitter Greens and Buffalo Mozzarella
laced with Lemon Shallot Vinaigrette

Sorbet
Granite of Raspberry

Entree
Grilled Breast of Pheasant with Mint Fig Chutney

Fried Polenta with Tomato Basil Coulis

Vegetable Ravioli

Dessert
Medley of Fresh Berries Accompanied with Ice Cream
and a Poached Pear

The Cincinnati Convention Center
&
Ogden Entertainment Services

Welcome P.C.M.A.

Fresh Mozzarella with Roma Tomatoes
Presented on Spring Mesclum
Finished with Balsamic Vinaigrette

Tenderloin of Beef and Spinach Pinwheels
with Morel Sauce

Breast of Chicken and Pepper Pinwheels
with Roasted Red Pepper Sauce

Filet of Fresh Sole with Mushroom and Onion Pinwheels
with Burre Blanc Sauce

Pear Potatoes

Zucchini Ring filled with Carrot Sticks

Belgium Chocolate with Vanilla Mousse
and Fresh Berries

Indiana Pork Producers Association

8902 Vincennes Circle, Suite F • Indianapolis, IN 46268 • (317) 872-7500 Fax (317) 872-6675

June 21, 1994

David Carter
Executive Chef
Crystal Catering
Governor Noble's Eating Place
13400 Allisonville Rd
Fishers, IN 46038

Dear David:

Thank you for your efforts in preparing the pork for the National Association of Nutrition and Aging Services Programs dinner at Conner Prairie. I appreciate your flexibility in using a new product as well as your professionalism in the presentation.

I have heard favorable reviews of the dinner and our participation. I owe thanks for these comments to you and your staff for their services.

I look forward to working with you again on future promotions. In the meantime, if I can be of any assistance, please give me a call.

Sincerely,

Sherrill M. Rude
Director of Marketing

SMR/kmc

enc.

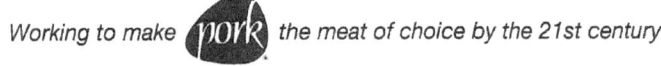

Certificate of Appreciation

This certificate is presented to

DAVID CARTER

on behalf of the Indiana Pork Producers Association
in recognition of his/her culinary talents and efforts to
"make pork the meat of choice by the 21st Century"

Given this __2ND__ day of __JUNE__ 19__94__

Tom Gusting
Marketing Chairman

Tony Hush
Executive Vice President

What is Gluten?

Gluten is a general name for the proteins found in wheat (durum, emmer, spelt, farina, faro, KAMUT®Khoras wheat and einkorn), rye, barley and tricale. Gluten helps foods maintain their shape, acting as a glue that holds food together.

The recipes' that follow in this section represent assorted ideas that meet the requirements for Gluten-free.

1. Slow-Cooker-Chinese Pork Tenderloin
2. Slow-Cooker-Pork chops a l' Orange
3. Slow-Cooker-Pork Roast with Fruit Medley
4. Fruit and Wheat Shredded
5. Quinoa Salad
6. Hummus Sandwich
7. Avocado, Pea and Radish Toast
8. Avocado and Strawberry Toast
9. Creamy Chocolate Pudding
10. Skillet Pork Chops with Butter Beans
11. Creole-Style Shrimp
12. Parchment Baked Halibut
13. Mediterranean Lentils
14. Cabbage and Carrot Salad with Peanut Sauce
15. Slow-Cooker-Wine Braised Brisket
16. Slow-Cooker-Greek Turkey Breast
17. *Gluten-Free Flour Mix* Information Page
18. Apple-Pistachio Crisp
19. Lobster, Crabmeat and Tortellini (Original Recipe by David)

GLUTEN INFORMATION

Calcium: broccoli, milk, yogurt, cheese, sardines with bone, collard greens, almonds

Iron: fish, meat, chicken, beans, nuts, seeds, eggs, amaranth, quinoa

Vitamin B: eggs, milk, meat, fish, orange juice, beans, nuts, seeds, gluten-free grains

Fiber: fruits, vegetable, and beans, full fat (not packaged shredded) unprocessed cheeses and plain yogurts

NOTE: Read labels. Check the product label to determine if the food was processed or packaged at a manufacturing facility with a potential gluten cross-contamination

GLUTEN-FREE FLOUR MIX

3 cups white rice flour

3 cups potato starch

2 cups sorghum flour

4 tsp. Xanthan gum (to stabilize mix)

In a large airtight container whisk, together all ingredients. Cover and store at room temperature for up to 3 months.

Seafood

1. Prawns and Pasta
2. Poached Salmon with White Beans
3. Mahi Mahi with Pineapple, Mango Salsa
4. Fiesta Tilapia with Saffron Rice
5. Red Snapper with Cumin Citrus Sauce
6. Broiled Curried Pollock
7. Grouper with Macadamia Nuts
8. Broiled Swordfish Steak
9. Louisiana Style Walleye Pike
10. Angel Hair Pasta with Salmon
11. Gulf Red Snapper En Papillote
12. Parmesan Baked Salmon
13. Chilean Sea Bass-Adriatic Style - Original Recipe by David
14. Mediterranean Cod
15. Pecan Crusted Halibut
16. Escargot Encroute
17. Hawaiian Cod by Lois
18. Swordfish with Cucumber, Red Pepper A'scapece
19. Cod with Capers and Onions
20. Snow Crab Linguini
21. Mixed Shellfish En Papillote
22. Salt Seared Sea Scallops
23. Snapper A'LaVeracruz
24. Catfish with Apple, Bacon Vinaigrette
25. Halibut Florentine
26. Cod in Tomato Sauce
27. Cucumber and Shrimp Salad
28. Asparagus and Scallops

Poultry

1. Cherry BBQ Chicken Drumsticks
2. Chicken Breast Stuffed with Goat Cheese
3. Chicken and Dressing Bake
4. Chicken Fingers with Honey Mustard
5. Chili Seasoned Grilled Chicken
6. Chicken Breast with Peppers and Sherry
7. Chicken with Coconut Apples by Debbie
8. Slow-Cooker-Teriyaki Chicken
9. Italian Style Chicken
10. Sun Dried Tomato Grilled Chicken
11. Brazo Chicken Sandwich-I.A.C.
12. Chicken Mandarin with Bananas
13. Cheesy Bacon Chicken with Mustard Sauce
14. Spanish Style Chicken and Mushrooms
15. Chicken Pignoli
16. Chicken Fettucine Cacciatore
17. Chicken and Mushroom Dinner
18. Almond Chicken Dijon
19. Chicken Fajitas by Mindy
20. Creamy Chicken Noodle Soup by Chano

Pork/Veal

1. Veal Porchettes
2. Pork Poivrade
3. Slow-Cooker-Baby Back Ribs
4. Veal Scaloppini with Mustard
5. Roasted Veal Chop with Mediterranean Salsa
6. Veal Chop Stuffed with Spinach and Cheese
7. Thin Pork with Cranberry Relish
8. Tomato and Spinach Toss
9. Sausage Crescent Cheese Balls
10. Pepper, Onion and Smoked Sausage
11. Pork Chops with Tomato Gravy by Brock
12. Prairie Pot Roast
13. Sausage and Tomato Rigatoni
14. Pork Chop Skillet with Pears
15. Bacon and Spinach Toss
16. Sausage and Apple Cornbread Stuffing

Beef/ Duck

1. Duck Breast A 'La Orange
2. Beef Bar-B-Que by Jack
3. Meaty Red Rice
4. Beef and Macaroni Casserole
5. Hungarian Beef Stew
6. Bruschetta Minute Steak
7. Slow-Cooker-Southwest Chili
8. Ultimate Grilled Steak
9. Rainbow Taco Salad (Walking Taco)
10. Homestyle Burger by Chano
11. Wine Braised Brisket with Onions (Slow Cooker)

Vegetables/Salads

1. A Sunday Flowerpot Salad
2. Kiwi and Papaya Salad
3. Braised Red Cabbage with Red Onions and Apples
4. Vegetarian Slow-Cooked Beans
5. Sweet and White Potato Spears
6. Spaghetti with Arugula, Tomato, Ricotta Salata
7. Sweet Potato Cakes
8. Arugula and Orange Salad
9. Mediterranean Lentils
10. Cabbage and Carrot Salad with Peanut Sauce
11. Angel Hair Pasta with tomato, Avocado

Sweets

1. Orange Stuff by Patty
2. Chocolate Peanut Butter Pie
3. German Chocolate Cheesecake Cake
4. Amaretto Delight
5. Chocolate Cinnamon Sherbet
6. Creamy Chocolate Pudding
7. Honey Bun Cake

Breakfast/ Lunch

1. Ultimate Omelet on English Muffin
2. Three Bears *Porridge*
3. Spanish Millet by Kimberly
4. Sesame Peanut Noodles
5. The Boardwalk Sandwich
6. Frittata with Bacon, Ricotta and Greens
7. Crust-less Bacon and Cheese Quiche

Sauces

1. White Sauces
2. Béchamel Sauce
3. Mornay Sauce- Cheese
4. Veloute Sauce
5. Easy Remoulade Sauce
6. Pommery Tarragon Sauce
7. Arugula Oil
8. Perigeaux Sauce
9. Sweet and Sour Sauce
10. Chile Butter

Index

1. Prawns and Pasta
2. Poached Salmon with White Beans
3. A Sunday Flowerpot Salad
4. Veal Porchettes
5. Orange Stuff by Patty
6. Sausage Crescent Cheese Balls
7. Slow-Cooker-Southwest Chili
8. Honey Bun Cake
9. Chocolate Peanut Butter Pie
10. Cherry BBQ Chicken Drumsticks
11. German Chocolate Cheesecake Cake
12. Slow-Cooker-Pork Chops A'l Orange
13. Slow-Cooker-Chinese Pork Tenderloin
14. Slow-Cooker-Pork roast with Fruit Medley
15. Fruit and Wheat
16. Quinoa Salad
17. Hummus Sandwich
18. Avocado, Pea and Radish Toast
19. Avocado and Strawberry Toast
20. Mahi Mahi with Pineapple, Mango Salsa
21. Amaretto Delight
22. Kiwi and Papaya Salad
23. Braised Red Cabbage with Red Onions and Apples
24. Fiesta Tilapia with Saffron Rice
25. Ultimate Omelet on English Muffin
26. Red Snapper with Cumin Citrus Sauce
27. Duck Breast A' la Orange
28. Pork Poivrade

29. Sausage and Apple Cornbread Stuffing
30. Chicken Breast Stuffed with Goat Cheese
31. Broiled Curried Pollock
32. Three Bears *Porridge*
33. Spanish Millet by Kimberly
34. Sesame Peanut Noodles
35. Grouper with Macadamia Nuts
36. Broiled Swordfish Steak
37. Rainbow Taco Salad (Walking Taco)
38. The Boardwalk Sandwich
39. Chicken and dressing Bake
40. Chicken Fingers with Honey Mustard
41. Louisiana Style Walleye Pike
42. Angel Hair Pasta with Salmon
43. Chili Seasoned Grilled Chicken
44. White Sauces
45. Béchamel Sauce
46. Mornay Sauce (Cheese)
47. Veloute' Sauce
48. Easy Remoulade Sauce
49. Beef Bar-B-Que by Jack
50. Meaty Red Rice
51. Vegetarian Slow-Cooked Beans
52. Slow-Cooker-Baby Back Ribs
53. Chicken Breast with Peppers and Sherry
54. Beef and Macaroni Casserole
55. Hungarian Beef Stew
56. Veal Scaloppini with Mustard
57. Roasted Veal Chop with Mediterranean Salsa
58. Gulf Red Snapper EnPalliote
59. Veal Chops Stuffed with Spinach and Cheese

60. Homestyle Burger by Chano
61. Chicken with Coconut Apples by Debbie
62. Parmesan Baked Salmon
63. Tomato and Spinach Toss
64. Slow-Cooker-Teriyaki Chicken
65. Italian Style Chicken
66. Chilean Sea Bass-Adriatic Style
67. Mediterranean Cod
68. Frittata with Bacon, Ricotta and greens
69. Sweet and White Potato Spears
70. Bacon and Spinach Pasta Toss
71. Pecan Crusted Halibut with Beurre Blanc Sauce
72. Sun Dried Tomato Grilled Chicken
73. Bruschetta Minute Steak
74. Brazo Chicken Sandwich-I.   A.   C.
75. Escargot Encroute
76. Chicken Mandarin with Bananas
77. Cheesy Bacon Chicken with Mustard Sauce
78. Pommery Tarragon Sauce
79. Hawaiian Cod by Lois
80. Asparagus and Scallops
81. Pork with Cranberry Relish
82. Swordfish with Cucumber, Red Pepper A'scapece
83. Cucumber and Shrimp Salad
84. Arugula Oil
85. Sweet Potato Cakes
86. Spaghetti with Arugula, Tomato, Ricotta Salata
87. Angel Hair Pasta with Tomato, Avocado
88. Cod with Capers and Onions
89. Snow Crab Linguini
90. Arugula and Orange Salad

91. Chocolate Cinnamon Sherbet
92. Perigeaux Sauce
93. Sweet and Sour Sauce
94. Mixed Shellfish En Papillote
95. Salt Seared Sea Scallops
96. Spanish Style Chicken and Mushrooms
97. Pepper, Onion and Smoked Sausage
98. Chile Butter
99. Chicken Pignoli
100. Snapper A La Veracruz
101. Pork Chops with Tomato Gravy by Brock
102. Catfish with apple, Bacon Vinaigrette
103. Ultimate Grilled steak
104. Crust less Bacon and Cheese Quiche
105. Chicken Fettuccine Cacciatore
106. Chicken and Mushroom Dinner
107. Almond Chicken Dijon
108. Prairie Land Pot Roast
109. Sausage and Tomato Rigatoni
110. Pork Chop Skillet with Pears
111. Halibut Florentine
112. Chicken Fajitas by Mindy
113. Creamy Chocolate Pudding
114. Skillet Pork Chops with Butter Beans
115. Creole-Style Shrimp
116. Parchment Baked Halibut
117. Mediterranean Lentils
118. Cabbage and Carrot Salad with Peanut Sauce
119. Slow-Cooker-Greek Turkey Breast
120. Cod in Tomato Sauce
121. Apple-Pistachio Crisp

122. Lobster, Crabmeat with Tortellini
123. Wine Braised Brisket with Onions (Slow Cooker)
124. Red Snapper with Cumin Citrus Sauce

PRAWNS AND PASTA

INGREDIENTS:

6 oz. jumbo shrimp-shell on
1 oz. cream sauce
2 oz. total fresh herbs, thyme, rosemary, Herb de Providence
3 oz. spinach linguini

1 tbsp. melted butter
1 tbsp. stick butter-cold
1 to 2 oz. white wine
2 oz. parmesan cheese shredded

DIRECTIONS:

1. Peel and devein shrimp-set aside
2. Make a cream sauce-see recipe
3. Sauté' shrimp in melted butter. Add herbs, when shrimp starts to change color pour in wine to deglaze the pan. Once drippings are loose, add cream sauce and cold butter to enhance the flavor.
4. Cook pasta according to directions
5. Place pasta on plate and garnish with parmesan cheese. Then arrange shrimp and pour sauce over the top.

POACHED SALMON ON A NEST OF WHITE BEANS

INGREDIENTS:

1 can (14.5oz.) white beans
½ cup fresh spinach
2 tbsp. diced tomato – fresh

2 ea. Lemon slice for garnish
2 oz. Rémoulade Sauce
4 to 6 oz. salmon filet

REMOULADE SAUCE

2 tbsp. mayonnaise
2 tbsp. chili sauce
1 tbsp. mustard, olive oil, hot sauce, lemon juice, Worcestershire sauce.
Mix together and hold

DIRECTIONS:

1. Heat white beans in a small pan, season to taste
2. Sauté' spinach in 2 tbsp. butter, season to taste
3. Fill shallow bowl or plate with beans
4. Poach salmon in seasoned water (white wine can also be used in water)
5. Place salmon in middle of beans, garnish edge with diced tomato and spinach
6. Put Remoulade Sauce over salmon

A SUNDAY FLOWERPOT SALAD

INGREDIENTS:

Yield approximately 16
4 lbs. Italian World blend lettuce
2 cups cherry tomatoes (cut in half)
8 oz. green pepper rings
4 oz. red onion rings (thin cut)
2 lbs. Jumbo ripe olives pitted (cut in half)
2 cups sliced radishes
2 cups shredded carrots
4 cups Feta Cheese crumbles
4 oz. diced green onions

20 oz. Extra Virgin Olive Oil
10 oz. Red wine vinegar
1 tbsp. Sea salt
1 tsp. Ground black pepper
1 oz. fresh garlic crushed
2 tbsp. whole leaf oregano
3 oz. sliced ripe olives – chopped fine
16 ea. 8 oz. glass flower pots or glass salad bowl

INSTRUCTIONS:

1. Place 1 cup of lettuce blend per glass flower pot
2. Layer with 8 ea. cherry tomato halves, 3 ea. Green pepper rings, 3 red onion rings and ¼ cup halved ripe olives
3. Make another layer with ½ cup of lettuce mix and scatter 2 tbsp. of sliced radishes on top
4. Add remainder of the ½ cup lettuce

5. Top with carrot, feta cheese and green onion
6. Serve with 2 oz. of Olivetti dressing on side or your choice of dressing
7. Dressing=oil, vinegar, salt, pepper, garlic, oregano and olives together and shake or whisk well
8. Note-Recipe makes one quart

ORANGE STUFF BY PATTY

This is great light desert and easy to make

1 cup cottage cheese (small or large curd)
3 cans Mandarin oranges
16 oz. low fat light cool whip
15 ea. Large box orange Jello mix
Optional - walnuts chopped or coconut

Mix all ingredients in a large bowl and chill until set

VEAL PORCHETTES

INGREDIENTS:

2 ea. Veal cutlets-4 oz. ea.
1 oz. diced ham
1 oz. Braised tomato concasse'
(braised stewed tomatoes)
1 ea. Slice of Romanoff Cheese
1 oz. Seasoned bread crumbs
1 tbsp. Parmesan cheese sprinkle to taste
6 oz. Tomato Pasta

INSTRUCTIONS:

1. Lightly pound 2 ea. Veal cutlets covered with plastic wrap
2. Flour and season to taste
3. Sauté' veal about 4 minutes on each side (1 tbsp. butter)
4. Braised Tomato concasse' - Recipe page#
5. Place sautéed veal on a pie shell or pan, add diced ham, Braised Tomato on top with cheese and seasoned bread crumbs
6. Place under a broiler until cheese melts.
7. Sprinkle with parmesan cheese
8. Follow directions for cooking pasta

SAUSAGE CRESCENT CHEESE BALLS

GREAT APPETIZER

INGREDIENTS:

1 lb. bulk spicy sausage (optional Chorizo)
2 cups shredded sharp cheddar cheese (8 oz.)
½ tsp. dried rosemary leaves crushed
1 can (8 oz.) refrigerated crescent dinner rolls
2 tbsp. all-purpose flour

DIRECTIONS:

1. Heat oven to 375*F, line 15x10x1 inch pan with foil; spray with cooking spray
2. In large bowl, mix sausage, cheese and rosemary; mix well using hands or spoon
3. Unroll crescent dough on work surface, coat each side of dough with 1 tbsp. flour. Using pizza cutter or knife, cut dough into about ¼ inch pieces. Mix crescent dough pieces into bowl of sausage mixture in small amounts until well blended.
4. Shape mixture into about 42 (1 ½ inch balls. Place in pan and bake 15 to 17 minutes or until golden brown.

SLOW COOKER SOUTHWEST CHILI

INGREDIENTS:

3 tbsp. vegetable oil
2 ea. medium onions diced
1 ea. Red bell pepper diced
6 ea. Cloves garlic chopped
2 small cans corn kernels- no salt and drain
¼ cup chili powder
2 lb. ground beef
1 lb. hot Italian sausage
1 ½ tsp. kosher salt
1 28oz. can diced tomatoes
1 can tomato paste
1 bottle of Lager (Sam Adams works very well)
1 cup beef broth
1 tbsp. light molasses
2 15 oz. cans kidney beans drain and rinse
4 small jalapeno chili peppers seeded, stemmed and diced
3 tbsp. minced chipotle peppers in adobo sauce

DIRECTIONS:

1. In a large skillet over medium heat, cook and break apart ground beef and sausage until done; drain excess grease off.
2. Combine the remaining ingredients in the slow cooker with meat.
3. Cook on low for 10 hours or on high for 4 hours. Please cover pot

HONEY BUN CAKE

INGREDIENTS:

1 cup brown sugar
1 yellow cake mix
2 cups powdered sugar
¾ cup vegetable oil
1 tbsp. milk

4 eggs
T tbsp. vanilla extract
8 oz. sour cream
2 tbsp. cinnamon

DIRECTIONS:

1. Mix cake mix, oil, eggs and sour cream by hand about 50 strokes.
2. Put half of mixture in a 9 x 13 baking pan
3. Combine brown sugar and cinnamon and spread over entire cake; then spread the rest of batter on top of this.
4. Using a knife make swirls in the cake batter
5. Bake at 325*F for about 40 min.
6. Blend powdered sugar, milk, vanilla and spread on warm cake; add milk until you reach a spreading consistency

CHOCOLATE PEANUT BUTTER PIE

INGREDIENTS:

1 chocolate graham pie crust
1 ½ pints vanilla ice cream, softened
2 cups creamy peanut butter (crunchy works)
1 container ice cream fudge topping (quick shell)
1 8 oz. whipped topping

DIRECTIONS:

1. Mix all ingredients ice cream, peanut butter and whipped topping. Put into the pie shell. Freeze for about 3 hours until firm. Once firm pour fudge topping over pie and return to freezer to set.

2. You can use mixer on low speed to blend ingredients. When ready to serve, remove from freezer and let sit for 10 to 15 minutes before cutting.

Revised from my first book

CHERRY BBQ CHICKEN DRUMSTICKS

INGREDIENTS:

3 tsp. ancho Chile powder
1 tsp. smoked paprika
Kosher salt and freshly ground black pepper- to taste
12 ea. Chicken drumsticks (about 4 lbs.)
2 tbsp. canola oil
1 ea. Vidalia onion finely chopped
2 cloves garlic chopped
2 tbsp. tomato paste

Juice of 2 oranges
Juice of 1 lemon
1 cup ketchup
1 (16 oz.) bag frozen pitted cherries, thawed
½ cup water
Oil for greasing grates for grilling
Fresh cherries for serving

DIRECTIONS:

1. In a small bowl, whisk 2 tsp. Chile powder, smoked paprika, 1 ½ tsp. salt
2. Add ½ tsp. black pepper. Season chicken and loosen the skin to season the meat. Cover with plastic wrap and marinate for at least one hour or overnight
3. Heat sauce pan to medium heat and add oil, onion, garlic and remaining 1 tsp. Ancho Chile powder, tomato paste.
4. Add orange juice, lemon juice, ketchup, cherries, water salt and pepper to taste.
5. Reduce heat to low and simmer for 30 minutes. Puree with a hand blender until smooth. Reserve 1 cup sauce for grilling, hold the rest for serving.
6. Preheat grill to medium heat. Oil grate, grill chicken until cooked and skin is crisp, about 25 minutes. Brush with reserved BBQ sauce and grill 5 min. more.

GERMAN CHOCOLATE CHEESECAKE CAKE

INGREDIENTS:

1 German chocolate cake mix prepared according to package directions adding the eggs, oil and water

Cream Cheese Filling

2- 8 oz. packages cream cheese, softened
1 ½ cups granulated sugar
4 eggs lightly beat

Coconut Pecan Frosting

1 cup granulated sugar
1 cup evaporated milk
½ cup butter, cubed (not margarine)
3 egg yolks, lightly beaten

1 tsp. vanilla extract
2 ½ cups flaked coconut
1 ½ cup chopped pecans

DIRECTIONS:

1. Prepare batter according to package directions, set batter aside. In a small bowl, beat cream cheese and sugar until smooth. Add eggs; beat on low speed just until combined.
2. Pour half of the cake batter into a greased and floured 13 x 9 in. baking dish. Gently pour cream cheese mixture over batter.
3. Spoon remaining batter over top; spread to edge of baking pan. Bake at 325*F for 65 to 75 minutes or until a toothpick comes out clean
4. Cool on a wire rack for 1 hour. Prepare frosting, in a heavy sauce pan, combine the sugar, milk, butter and egg yolks.
5. Cook and stir over medium low heat until thickened and a thermometer reads 160* or is thick to coat the back of metal spoon.
6. Remove from heat. Stir in vanilla; fold in coconut and pecans. Cool until frosting reaches spreading consistency.
7. Frost cooled cake and refrigerate

Serves about 14-16

SLOW-COOKER PORK CHOPS A L'ORANGE

INGREDIENTS:

2 tbsp. extra virgin olive oil
8 bone-in pork chops
½ cup orange juice
2 tbsp. clover honey
1 tsp. salt
1 tsp. packed brown sugar

1 tsp. grated orange peel
¼ cup water
2 tbsp. cornstarch
Suggested serving with rice

DIRECTIONS:

1. Heat oil in a large skillet over medium-high heat. Add pork in batches; cook 5 to 7 minutes on each side or until browned.
2. Combine orange juice, honey, salt, brown sugar and orange peel in crock-pot slow cooker. Add pork; turn to coat. Cover; cook on low 6 to 8 hours.
3. Remove pork to a plate. Stir water into cornstarch in a small bowl until smooth; whisk into cooking liquid. Cover; cook on low 15 minutes or until thickened
4. Serve sauce over pork and rice
5. Garnish with orange slice twist
6. Note: Trim excess fat from chops to reduce fat while cooking

SLOW-COOKER CHINESE PORK TENDERLOIN

INGREDIENTS:

2 pork tenderloins (1-2lbs. total), cut into 1 inch cubes
1 jar (15 oz.) gluten-free sweet and sour sauce
1 green bell pepper, cut into ½ in. pieces
1 red bell pepper, cut into ½ in. pieces
1 onion, thinly sliced
2 carrots, thinly sliced
1 tbsp. gluten-free soy sauce
½ tsp. hot pepper sauce
Hot cooked rice, garnish with cilantro

DIRECTIONS:

Place pork, sweet and sour sauce, bell peppers, onion, carrots, soy sauce and hot pepper sauce into slow cooker; stir until well blended. Cover; cook on low 6 to 7 hours or on high 4 to 5 hours. Serve over rice. Garnish with cilantro

SLOW-COOKER PORK ROAST WITH FRUIT MEDLEY

INGREDIENTS:

1 Cup water
½ cup kosher or coarse salt
2 tbsp. sugar
1 tsp. dried thyme
2 whole bay leaves
1 boneless pork roast (about 2-4 lbs.)
Olive oil
2 cups green seedless grapes

1 cup dried apricots
1 cup dried plums
1 cup red wine
2 cloves garlic, minced
Juice of ½ lemon

DIRECTIONS:

1. Combine water, salt, sugar, thyme and bay leaves in a large resealable food storage bag. Add roast. Marinate overnight or up to 2 days in refrigerator. Turning meat.
2. Remove roast from marinade; pat dry. Heat oil in a large skillet over medium heat. Add roast; cook 5 to 7 minutes or until browned on all sides. Transfer to slow cooker.
3. Add grapes, apricots plums, wine, garlic and lemon juice; stir to combine. Cover; cook on low 7 to 9 hours or high 3 to 5 hours.
4. Remove pork slice and serve sauce over meat

FRUIT AND WHEAT

Combine ½ cup shredded wheat, ½ cup strawberries slice, ½ banana sliced, 2 tbsp. Ground flaxseed, and 1 tbsp. walnuts in bowl. Top with ¾ cup unsweetened soy milk.

QUINOA SALAD

Toss 4 cups cooked quinoa with 1 can (10 oz.) artichoke hearts, drained and chopped; 1 cup cooked corn kernels; 1 cup grape tomatoes, halved; ¾ cup cooked edamame; 1 bell pepper (green, red, yellow or orange) diced.

Whisk 4 tbsp. olive oil; 2 tbsp. lime juice; 1 clove garlic, mince; ¼ tsp. ground cumin; ¼ tsp. coriander; and ¼ tsp. salt. Toss dressing with quinoa mixture and top with fresh basil

HUMMUS SANDWICH

Top 1 slice whole grain bread with ¼ cup hummus; 1 slices of tomato; and ½ avocado sliced. Drizzle with olive oil and season with salt and pepper to taste.

Top with another slice whole grain bread.

AVOCADO TOAST

AVOCADO AND STRAWBERRY TOAST

Mash 1 small avocado with 1 tsp. lime juice and spread over 2 slices toasted whole grain bread. Top each toast with 2 sliced strawberries and 2 tsp. honey

AVOCADO, PEAS AND RADISH TOAST

Mash 1 small avocado and spread over 2 slices of toasted whole grain bread. Top each toast with 1 tbsp. goat cheese; 1 radish sliced; 1 tbsp. frozen and thawed peas; a drizzle of extra virgin olive oil.

AVOCADOS

Avocados contain monounsaturated fatty acids(MUFAs)

Some noted benefits: Research Studies

1. Helps melt stubborn belly fat and keep it off
2. Good source of lutein and antioxidant that promotes eye health
3. May boost memory and prevent mental decline.
4. An avocado could cut bad cholesterol
5. Studies show that MUFA- rich diets help regulate blood sugar levels just as effectively as conventional low-fat diets, reducing diabetes risk.

Note: Source: Prevention.Com August 2015

MAHI WITH PINEAPPLE, MANGO SALSA

INGREDIENTS:

2 ea. 4 oz. Mahi filets
1 cup pineapple diced
1 cup mango diced
2 tsp. onion diced (sweet)
1 tsp. rosemary chopped
3 tbsp. white wine vinegar
3 tbsp. sugar
2 tbsp. white wine

Salt and pepper to taste
T tsp. onion powder
1 tsp. garlic powder
1 tsp. ground black pepper
1 cup flour
¼ cup vegetable oil or olive oil

DIRECTIONS:

1. Lightly flour Mahi filets
2. Add seasoning to flour
3. 3. Use oil in large skillet and sauté filets until firm about 4 min. on each side; sprinkle with rosemary
4. Mix all fruit, onion, white wine vinegar, sugar, white wine. Mix in large bowl and set aside to let flavors blend.
5. After fish has been cooked on both sides, add fruit mixture to deglaze pan and simmer for about 3 min.

Serves - 2

AMARETTO DELIGHT

INGREDIENTS:

2 scoops of Amaretto ice cream
1 tsp. chocolate syrup
1 tsp. honey
½ cup milk

Put all ingredients into a blender and mix thoroughly. Fill a wine glass with mixture and put into freezer for about 10-15 min. to form a milkshake.

Top with whip cream and cherry if desired.

Note: If unable to find amaretto ice cream, add amaretto syrup to ice cream

KIWI AND PAPAYA SALAD WITH LIME CORIANDER DRESSING

INGREDIENTS:

1 ea. Papaya, peeled, seeded and cut into slices
2 ea. Kiwi fruit, peeled, pitted and sliced
1 ea. Purple kale, for garnish
1 ea. Lime cut into wedges for garnish

*Lime Coriander Dressing
1 ea. Egg yolk
1 tbsp. ground coriander
2 tbsp. lime juice(fresh)
¾ cup extra virgin olive oil
1 tbsp. of honey (to taste)
¼ tsp. ground black pepper

Whisk together egg yolk and lime juice in a bowl. Slowly whisk in oil and season with coriander, honey, salt and pepper.

PLATE:

1. Place alternating slices of kiwi fruit and papaya on salad plate lined with purple kale.
2. Drizzle dressing across fruit and garnish with lime wedges

BRAISED RED CABBAGE WITH RED ONION AND APPLES

INGREDIENTS:

2 tbsp. vegetable oil
1 ½ cups red onions, chopped
8 cups red cabbage, thinly sliced
2 cloves garlic minced
2 apples, peeled, cored, and chopped

1 cup chicken stock
¼ cup red wine vinegar
2 tbsp. brown sugar
1 ea. Bay leaf
Salt and pepper to taste

DIRECTIONS:

1. In a large skillet with a lid place vegetable oil to heat
2. Put cabbage in skillet to start the breakdown.
3. Add red onions, garlic, apples, chicken stock, red wine vinegar, brown sugar, bay leaf, salt and pepper to taste.
4. Put lid on to start braising approximately 15- 20 min.
5. Remove bay leaf before serving

FIESTA TILAPIA WITH SAFFRON RICE

INGREDIENTS:

1 10oz. package saffron rice
¼ cup garlic chopped
1 ea. Green bell pepper, chopped or 5 to 7 jalapeno Chile peppers seeded and chopped
2 ea. Roma tomatoes, chopped
½ cup red onions or Spanish onions chopped
1/3 cup Cilantro chopped
1 tsp. salt, 1 tsp. pepper
¼ cup olive oil
1 or 2 lemon or limes (will need 6 tbsp. juice)
4 ea. Tilapia filets

DIRECTIONS:

1. Thaw fish and rinse then pat dry with paper towel
2. Season fish to your taste (we use onion powder, garlic, ground black pepper)
3. Prepare the rice using the package directions
4. Combine the garlic, bell pepper, tomatoes, onion, cilantro, salt, pepper and the olive oil; mix well. Add lemon juice
5. Arrange fish in a baking dish so sides do not touch
6. Spoon the tomato mixture over each fish.
7. Bake at 350*F covered with foil for 18 to 25 minutes or until fish flakes easily
8. Serve with rice

ULTIMATE OMELETE ON ENGLISH MUFFIN

INGREDIENTS:

2 ea. English muffin
1 round cookie cutter-3 in.
1 cup onion, pepper medley-frozen
5 eggs - whipped
½ cup diced ham

¼ cup shredded cheddar cheese - to taste
1 tsp. onion powder, garlic powder, black pepper
2 tbsp. oil

DIRECTIONS:

1. Heat oil in skillet over medium high heat
2. Add onion medley, diced ham and seasoning; cook until medley starts to become transparent.
3. Pour egg mixture over medley making sure all is covered.
4. Cook until egg sets- shaking pan to keep it from sticking (may need to use spatula to move egg)
5. Lightly toast muffin
6. Once egg has set, use cookie cutter to make circle and place on top of muffin side
7. Top with cheddar cheese and remaining top of muffin

RED SNAPPER WITH CUMIN CITRUS SAUCE

INGREDIENTS:

6 oz. Red Snapper filet
2 tbsp. vegetable oil or virgin olive oil
2 tsp. onion powder
2 tsp. garlic powder
Salt and pepper to taste
2 tbsp. flour

CUMIN CITRUS SAUCE

2 oz. orange juice
2 oz. soy sauce
1 tsp. cumin

DIRECTIONS:

1. Heat oil in skillet on medium high heat
2. Season fish on both sides
3. Lightly season flour and put fish in mixture- shake excess off
4. Mix ingredients for cumin citrus sauce in a small bowl
5. Cook fish until browned both sides. Remove fish and add sauce to pan and stir to blend; add fish back and cook 2 minutes more.
6. Serve fish and spoon sauce over top

DUCK BREAST A LA' ORANGE

INGREDIENTS:

2 ea. Duck breast (4 to 6oz ea.)
1 tbsp. orange marmalade
¼ cup orange juice (mix these two ingredients and stir for marinade); add duck breast in a reseal able bag; marinate 1 to 2 hours or over night
1 tsp. onion powder
1 tsp. garlic powder
1 tsp. black pepper
Salt and pepper to taste
2 tbsp. vegetable oil
2 oz. cream sauce
1 to 2 oz. Cointreau or any orange liquor
1 ea. Orange

DIRECTIONS:

1. Heat oil in skillet on medium high heat
2. Season Duck breast on both sides (onion, garlic, pepper)
3. Mix cream sauce and Cointreau and hold
4. Cook breast skin side up to brown; then turn to brown and crisp skin side
5. Remove breast; side aside. Then add cream sauce mixture to pan, stirring well.
6. Add breast back to pan and simmer about 10 minutes, until breast is firm (165*F)
7. Serve pouring sauce over top of breast
8. Garnish with orange zest and orange wedges

PORK POIVRADE

The term Poivrade usually suggest that Game, Venison could be substituted in this recipe, but pork takes the treatment well.

INGREDIENTS:

- 4 lb. boneless pork shoulder
- 3 tbsp. peppercorns
- 2 ea. Carrots - sliced
- 1 large onion slice
- 10 ea. Juniper berries
- 3 cups red wine
- ¾ cup red wine vinegar
- 1 ½ cups white veal or chicken stock
- 2 tbsp. butter
- 1/3 cup flour
- 3 tbsp. red currant jelly
- Salt and pepper to taste
- 3 tbsp. chopped chives

DIRECTIONS:

1. Trim excess fat sinew from pork and cut into large chunks. Place meat, 1tbsp. of peppercorns, the carrots, sliced onion, juniper berries, wine, and vinegar into heavy bottomed pan.
2. Bring the liquid to a boil and simmer, uncovered for one hour. Add stock to keep meat always covered.
3. Remove meat, strain cooking liquid and save. Crush remaining peppercorns; melt butter in pan, add pepper and flour. Cook slowly until flour browns.
4. Whisk in the strained cooking liquid and bring to a boil. Reduce heat, stir in jelly and add pork. Simmer until meat is tender about 40 minutes. Adjust seasoning if necessary.

SAUSAGE AND APPLE CORNBREAD STUFFING

INGREDIENTS:

1 - lb. pure pork sausage
½ cup chopped onion
½ cup chopped celery
1 cup chopped, peeled and cored tart green apples
½ cup turkey broth

1 large egg beaten
1 tsp. dried thyme leaves
½ tsp. ground sage
1 package (8oz.) cornbread stuffing

DIRECTIONS:

1. Break up sausage into a large skillet; cook over moderately high heat, stirring often to break up pieces. Remove sausage with a slotted spoon and reserve
2. Add onion, celery and apple to skillet; sauté' until just tender. Remove from heat and stir in broth, egg, thyme and sage.
3. Add sausage and cornbread stuffing and toss until well blended.
4. Stuff into turkey, whole chicken, pork roast.
5. This could be baked as a side, just add more broth and cover with foil; bake for about 1 hour.

CHICKEN BREAST STUFFED WITH GOAT CHEESE WRAPPED IN PROSCIUTTO HAM

INGREDIENTS:

2 oz. spinach fresh
6 oz. chicken breast
2 to 3 oz. Goat cheese/ Gouda cheese
2 to 3 slices prosciutto ham
Chopped parsley for garnish

Diced tomato
1 oz. vodka
2 tbsp. fresh basil
Salt and pepper to taste

DIRECTIONS:

1. Slice thick side of breast almost through or pound out chicken breast using plastic wrap
2. Place cheese and spinach inside and fold over to close
3. Wrap chicken breast with the slices of prosciutto and put on baking pan
4. Heat oven to 375*F, bake the chicken for about 1 hour/ until internal temp reaches 165*F
5. Make salsa of tomato, vodka and fresh basil/ mix diced tomato, basil, vodka, salt and pepper to taste; let it set to blend flavors
6. Serve chicken on top of tomato mixture
7. Note: a cream sauce can be used also.

BROILED CURRIED POLLOCK

INGREDIENTS:

2 ea. Pollock filets
2 tbsp. honey
2 tbsp. spicy mustard

2 tbsp. lemon juice (prefer fresh)
1 tbsp. curry powder
½ tsp. salt

DIRECTIONS:

1. Thaw Pollack and pat dry with a paper towel
2. Put thawed fish on a plate and season to taste
3. Mix the remaining ingredients and spread on both sides of the fish. Let stand for 15 minutes.
4. Place seasoned fish on broil pan and broil 4 inches from heat about 10 minutes or until fish flakes easily with a fork. Do not turn the fish
5. Serve over Jasmine rice with scallions

Note: can be baked uncovered 13 to 18 min at 350* degrees

THREE BEARS *PORRIDGE*

Rolled oats, gluten-free example Semolina, rice, wheat, barley. The ultimate winter Breakfast

INGREDIENTS:

2 large ripe bananas, peeled and mashed well (3/4 cup)
2 medium carrots, peeled and grated (3/4 cup)
1 cup rolled oats, certified gluten-free
2 ¼ cups water or milk of your choice
2 tbsp. chia seeds
Dash of sea salt
1 ½ tsp. cinnamon to taste

DIRECTIONS:

1. Place mashed banana into medium pot, add grated carrots
2. Add rolled oats with water or milk, chia seeds, salt. Stir well until blended
3. Heat on low then increase heat to medium.
4. Cook the oats uncovered, stirring for about 10 to 15 minutes, until oats are soft and mixture is thick
5. Note: you could mix and refrigerate overnight, then just simply heat it and serve
6. If mixture gets to thick, add a little water or milk

SPANISH MILLET PAELLA BY KIMBERLY

INGREDIENTS:

2 cups Millet (Vegetarian food, any of various small seeded annual cereal and forage grasses)
A few Saffron threads
1 cup yellow onion, diced
2 cloves garlic, minced
½ cup diced scallions
1 medium red bell pepper, diced

5 cups diced fresh tomatoes
½ lb. sugar snap peas
Sea salt to taste
6 cups vegetable broth

DIRECTIONS:

1. Soak millet overnight then rinse
2. Heat ¼ cup vegetable broth, medium heat; add saffron
3. Add onion, garlic, scallions and cook until onion is soft
4. Add peppers, millet; cook and to stir mix.
5. Add 5 cups of vegetable stock and reduce heat. Cook about 18 minutes or until millet has softened. Stirring
6. Stir in tomatoes and snap peas. Cover pot and cook about 5 minutes. Until millet is al dente' and snap peas are soft
7. The paella should retain creamy risotto-like texture from the broth. Add salt to taste

SESAME PEANUT NOODLES

INGREDIENTS:

1 lb. whole wheat spaghetti
1 red bell pepper, strips
2 tbsp. thinly sliced water chestnuts
1 carrot, cut into matchsticks
½ cup smooth natural peanut butter
¼ cup rice vinegar
¼ cup reduced sodium soy sauce
2 tbsp. lime juice
1 tbsp. extra virgin olive oil
1 tbsp. honey
2 tsp. dark sesame oil
2 tsp. grated ginger
1 tsp. sea salt

DIRECTIONS:

1. Cook spaghetti according to package directions (al dente')
2. Mix all the other ingredients together in bowl, stirring well
3. Toss pasta with the other ingredients
4. Top with 1 tbsp. toasted sesame seeds

GROUPER WITH MACADAMIA NUTS

INGREDIENTS:

1 ea. Grouper filet
3 to 4 oz. Macadamia nuts
Pineapple salsa- 1 cup diced pineapple, ¼ cup mandarin oranges, red seedless grapes mix well-note grapefruit segments can be substituted for pineapple diced
1 cup Orzo pasta
2 tbsp. flour

2 tsp. onion powder
2 tsp. garlic powder
2 tsp. black pepper
2 tbsp. vegetable oil or olive oil

DIRECTIONS:

1. Mix flour with seasonings
2. Put fish in flour mixture and coat both sides
3. Sauté' with oil in skillet until brown on both sides
4. Remove fish and place on a broiler pan with crushed macadamia nuts.
5. Broil about 4 inches from heat
6. Serve with Orzo pasta and lemon wedge
7. Put salsa next to fish.

BROILED SWORDFISH STEAK

INGREDIENTS:

6 to 8 oz. Swordfish steak
2 tbsp. onion powder
2 tbsp. garlic powder

2 tbsp. black pepper
Salt and pepper to taste
2 tbsp. Sundried Tomato Dressing

DIRECTIONS:

Marinate fish in the Sundried Tomato Dressing; mix seasonings together and pat on both sides of fish. Place on broiler pan about 4 in. from heat. Do not turn the fish. For about 15 minutes. Fish is done when firm to touch

Option: Marinade fish in Sundried Tomato Dressing before broiling or

2 tsp. Dijon mustard
1 tsp. mustard seeds

Brush both sides of fish with mustard and seeds. Place on broiler about 4 in. from heat. Turn fish and broil on the other side 4-5 min.

RAINBOW TACO SALAD

(WALKING TACO)

INGREDIENTS:

1 lb. ground turkey
1 package Taco seasoning mix
2 package Cheese Tortilla Chip snack bags
½ cup shredded lettuce
½ cup diced tomatoes
½ cup diced avocado

1 small can sweet corn – 1 tsp. per serving
1 small can black beans – 1 tsp. per serving
¼ cup shredded sharp cheddar cheese – 1 tsp. per serving

DIRECTIONS:

1. Brown turkey in a medium skillet over medium heat; Drain any excess grease. Add taco seasoning and prepare according to package instructions
2. Open desired bags of chips and add ¼ cup cooked meat to each bag
3. Top with lettuce, tomatoes, avocado, corn, beans and cheese
4. Top with a spoon of sour cream, optional

THE BOARDWALK SANDWICH

"THE GENERAL'S FAVORITE"

INGREDIENTS:

6 oz. sliced breast of turkey
2 oz. shredded lettuce
1 oz. 1000 Island Dressing
1 ea. Tomato, sliced

1 ea. Hardboiled egg sliced
4 ea. Strips of cooked bacon
1 ea. White toast
Served open face

DIRECTIONS:

Assemble as listed

White toast

1000 island dressing

Sliced turkey

Shredded lettuce

Tomato

Hardboiled egg

Bacon slice

CHICKEN AND DRESSING BAKE

INGREDIENTS:

¼ cup flour
1 tsp. salt
½ tsp. paprika
¼ tsp. pepper
1 ¾ lbs. chicken thighs (5 thighs)
2 to 4 tbsp. oil shortening
1 ½ cups chopped celery

¼ cup instant minced onion or ½ cup chopped onion
7 cups (7 oz. pkg.) seasoned bread stuffing cubes
Optional: poultry seasoning or thyme to taste
1 ¼ cup (10 ½ oz. can) condensed cream of chicken soup
1 ½ cup water

DIRECTIONS:

1. Preheat oven to 375*F
2. In a plastic bag, combine flour, salt, paprika and pepper. Shake chicken pieces, two or three at a time to coat.
3. In a large heavy fry pan over medium heat, brown chicken pieces well in hot oil. Remove chicken and set aside.
4. Sprinkle celery and onion in a 13 x 9-inch baking dish. Top with stuffing cubes.
5. In a mixing bowl combine soup and water; pour mixture evenly over cubes. Then arrange chicken over stuffing. Cover with foil; bake at 375* for 45 to 55 minutes until chicken is tender

CHICKEN FINGERS WITH HONEY MUSTARD

INGREDIENTS:

4 ea. 4 oz. skinless, boneless chicken breast
1 cup flour
½ tsp. salt
¼ tsp. cracked black pepper
¾ cup milk
1 cup oil

Homey Mustard Dipping Sauce:

½ cup honey
¼ cup Dijon mustard – Mix well together and set aside

DIRECTIONS:

1. Cut chicken into ½ x 2 inch strips
2. Mix flour, salt and pepper in a shallow bowl. Dip chicken in milk; put chicken flour next, cover well. Put chicken on wax paper.
3. Put about 2 to 3 tbsp. of oil in large heavy skillet.
4. Divide chicken into batches. Place chicken in an even layer in hot oil. Fry turning once, for about 3 minutes on each side or until golden brown.
5. Drain on paper towels. Repeat for remaining chicken
6. Serve dipping sauce on side

Note: make sure chicken is cooked well

LOUISIANA STYLE WALLEYE PIKE

INGREDIENTS:

1 6 oz. Walleye Pike filet
2 tbsp. oil
2 tbsp. Cajun seasoning
2 ea. Jalapeno peppers – cut and seeded
Salt and pepper to taste
1 tsp. cumin optional

1 tsp. garlic powder
1 tsp. onion powder
1 tsp. black pepper
1 tsp. Cayenne pepper
1 tsp. Crushed red pepper flakes optional (more heat)

DIRECTIONS:

1. heat oil in a heavy skillet to medium high
2. Season filet with skin side down with all the seasoning
3. Place filet in skillet gently with skin side down and cook, about 3 to 4 minutes. Check fish to see if seasoning is browned. Turn fish over and cook 1 to 3 minutes more
4. Garnish with Jalapeno peppers on side

Note: Crushed red pepper optional on top

ANGEL HAIR PASTA WITH SALMON

INGREDIENTS:

2 tbsp. olive oil
1 4 oz. salmon filets-cut into cubes
1 carrot slice diagonally
1 (10 oz.) package frozen broccoli, thawed
2 cloves garlic, minced

12 oz. angel hair pasta
2/3 cup chicken broth
1 tsp. dried basil
¼ cup grated Parmesan cheese

DIRECTIONS:

1. Heat 1 tbsp. oil in medium skillet; add salmon cubes. Cook, stirring well until salmon firms up and is cooked through, about 5 to 6 minutes. Remove from skillet and place on paper towels.
2. Add 1 tbsp. oil in same skillet. Add carrot to skillet, stir for about 4 minutes; add broccoli and garlic to skillet, cook stirring for 2 to 3 minutes longer.
3. Cook pasta according to package directions.
4. Add chicken broth to skillet, basil and parmesan cheese. Stir to combine and add salmon. Lower heat and simmer 4 to 6 min.
5. Drain pasta. Put on plates and top with salmon vegetable mixture.

CHILI SEASONED GRILLED CHICKEN

INGREDIENTS:

1 ½ cups chili sauce
¾ cup red wine vinegar
1 ½ tbsp. prepared horseradish
2 cloves garlic, chopped
1 tsp. salt
4ea. 4 to 6oz. chicken breast- bone-in

DIRECTIONS:

1. Mix chili sauce, vinegar, horseradish, garlic and salt in a bowl. Put ½ of the marinade in another bowl for basting.
2. Add chicken to bowl; turn to coat. Cover and marinate in refrigerator for at least 10 min. or overnight.
3. Preheat grill or broiler. Remove chicken from marinade and place on grill or broiler pan.
4. Grill or broil chicken, turning and basting often with reserved marinade. (Note: throw marinade chicken was in away)
5. Chicken by piercing with a knife or 165* internal temp. About 30 to 40 minutes depending on heat of grill.
6. Warm remaining reserved marinade, serve with chicken.

WHITE SAUCES

(SAUCE Blanche)

INGREDIENTS:

tbsp. butter
3 tbsp. flour
2 cups milk
Salt and pepper to taste

DIRECTIONS:

1. Melt the butter in a sauce pan and add flour, stirring with a wire whisk. Add milk, stirring rapidly. Cook, stirring about 5 minutes until thickened and smooth. Season to taste with salt and pepper. Yield 2 cups

SAUCE BECHAMEL

(FLAVORED WHITE SAUCE)

INGREDIENTS:

2 cups milk
1 ea. sliced onion
6 ea. Peppercorns
1 ea. Bay leaf
1/8 tsp. ground mace

3 tbsp. butter
3 tbsp. flour
Salt and pepper to taste

DIRECTIONS:

1. Pour the milk into a sauce pan and add the onion, peppercorn, bay leaf and mace. Cover the pan and heat the milk until almost boiling. Remove from heat and let set 5 to 7 minutes. Strain and discard the flavorings.

2. Melt butter in the cleaned-out sauce pan and add the flour, stirring with a wire whisk. Add the milk, stirring rapidly. Cook, stirring about 5 minutes until thickened and smooth. Season to taste with salt and pepper.

CHEESE SAUCE

(SAUCE MORNAY)

Add ½ to 1 cup grated cheese, preferably, Gruyere or Swiss, to the finished white or flavored white sauce and stir until smooth

VELOUTE' SAUCE

INGREDIENTS:

1 ½ tbsp. butter
1 ½ tbsp. flour
1 ¼ cups chicken broth
¼ cup light cream

1 egg yolk
2 tbsp. heavy cream
Fresh squeezed lemon juice and salt, pepper to taste

DIRECTIONS:

1. Melt butter in a sauce pan and add flour, stirring with a wire whisk. Add the broth, stirring rapidly; add the light cream, bring to a boil and let cook about 5 minutes or until syrupy.
2. Lightly beat the egg yolk with heavy cream; stir in lemon juice and salt, pepper to taste. Add to pan. Do not allow to boil or sauce will curdle.

Yield 2 cups

EASY REMOULADE SAUCE

1 cup mayonnaise, add 2 tsp. red wine vinegar, then add 3 tbsp. sweet relish, 2 tsp. chopped fresh tarragon or ½ tsp. dried tarragon. Season to taste with salt and pepper then blend well. Horseradish can be used instead of relish. I have also used tartar sauce as an option.

BEEF BAR-B-QUE BY JACK

INGREDIENTS:

2 to 3 lb. of ground beef
1 to 3 medium yellow onions, diced
Cook in a large skillet- season to taste- Pour off grease before mixing with the sauce
1 can tomato soup
1 bottle catsup
1 bottle chili sauce
1 bottle cocktail sauce
2 tbsp. mustard
2 tbsp. vinegar
2 tbsp. sugar
2 tbsp. Worcestershire sauce

DIRECTIONS:

Mix in a large sauce pan, meat, onions and all other ingredients; bring to a boil for about 10 minutes and reduce heat. Simmer with lid about 10 to 15 minutes.

Best after being refrigerated and reheated.

Note: Sauce and meat will blend well overnight

Can be served on a bun or open face on toast

MEATY RED RICE

INGREDIENTS:

1 tbsp. vegetable oil
1 lb. ground Italian sausage
1 (16 oz.) pack of smoked sausage, diced
2 (10 oz.) cans original Diced Tomatoes with green chilies, drained

1 sm. Red onion, diced
3 cups chicken broth
2 ½ tsp. creole seasoning
1 ½ cups long grain rice

DIRECTIONS:

1. Heat a large pot over medium high heat, add oil and brown ground sausage. Add smoked sausage and cook until brown. Add red onion and cook until soft about 3 min.
2. Stir in tomato with chilies, broth and creole seasoning and bring to a boil.
3. Stir in rice and bring to a boil
4. Cover and reduce heat to low; simmer for 25 min. or until all liquid is absorbed.
5. Fluff rice with a fork and serve hot

VEGETARIAN SLOW-COOKED BEANS

INGREDIENTS:

4 cans (15 ½ oz. ea.) Great northern beans, rinsed and drained
4 medium carrots, finely chopped
1 cup vegetable stock
6 ea. Garlic cloves, minced
2 tsp. ground cumin
2 tsp. Herbs de Provence
¼ tsp salt
1/8 tsp. chili powder

4 cups fresh baby spinach, coarsely chopped
1 cup oil-packed sun dried tomatoes, pat dry and chop
1/3 cup minced fresh cilantro
1/3 cup minced fresh parsley
2 cups chopped fresh kale

DIRECTIONS:

In a 3 to 4-quart slow cooker, combine the first eight ingredients. Cook, covered, on low 4 to 5 hours or until carrots are tender, adding spinach, kale, and tomatoes during the last 10-15 min.; stir in cilantro and parsley.

Serve Hot

SLOW COOKER BABY BACK RIBS

INGREDIENTS:

2 tbsp. smoked paprika
2 tsp. chili powder
2 tsp. garlic salt
1 tsp. onion powder

1 tsp. black pepper cracked
½ tsp. cayenne pepper
4 lbs. pork baby back ribs

SAUCE:

½ cup each mayonnaise, Worcestershire sauce and yellow mustard
¼ cup low sodium soy sauce
3 to 4 tbsp. hot pepper sauce or Sriracha sauce

DIRECTIONS:

1. In a small bowl, combine the first six ingredients. Cut ribs into serving - size pieces; rub with seasoning mixture. Marinate overnight. Place ribs in a 6-qt. slow cooker. Cook, covered, on low 5-6 hours or until meat is tender

2. Preheat oven to 375*. In a small bowl, whisk the sauce ingredients. Transfer ribs to a foil lined 15x10x1 in. baking pan; brush with some of the sauce. Bake 15 to 20 minutes or until browned, turning once and brushing occasionally with sauce. Serve with remaining sauce

CHICKEN BREAST WITH PEPPERS AND SHERRY

INGREDIENTS:

4 ea. Whole skinless, boneless chicken breast
Salt and pepper to taste
2 tbsp. Herb de Provence
4 ea. Peppers (red and green combined)

2 tbsp. butter
2 tbsp. chopped red onions or shallots
½ cup dry sherry
½ cup heavy cream

DIRECTIONS:

1. Sprinkle the chicken with salt and pepper, Herb de Provence. Shape into ovals
2. Cut the peppers lengthwise into thin strips.
3. Heat the butter in a heavy casserole. Add the chicken and cook, turning occasionally, about 5 minutes. Scatter the pepper strips and shallots around the chicken; cover and cook another 5 minutes.
4. Sprinkle the mixture with the sherry. Cover and continue cooking about 15 minutes. Turn the chicken and stir the pepper strips to cook evenly
5. Move the chicken to serving platter and keep hot.
6. Add the cream to the peppers in the casserole. Season to taste. Cook, uncovered, about 5 minutes to reduce the cream in half.
7. Spoon or ladle peppers and cream sauce over chicken.

Note: Make sure the chicken is done 165*F

BEEF AND MACARONI CASSEROLE

INGREDIENTS:

1 ½ cups elbow macaroni
3 ½ tbsp. butter
¾ cup diced onion
¼ cup diced green bell pepper
1 lb. ground chuck
1 tsp. dried basil
1 tsp. dried oregano
1 can drained diced tomatoes

3 tbsp. flour
2 cups milk
10 oz. cheddar cheese cubed
¼ tsp. grated nutmeg
Salt and pepper to taste
¼ tsp. cayenne pepper
Grated parmesan cheese to cover top

DIRECTIONS:

1. Preheat the oven to 450*F
2. Drop the macaroni into boiling salted water; simmer until barely tender (aldente'). Drain and rinse under cold running water.
3. Heat 1 ½ tbsp. butter in a skillet and add the onion and green pepper. Cook, stirring, until onion is wilted. Add the beef and cook, stirring, until no longer reddish. Drain off excess fat. Add the basil, oregano and tomatoes. Stir and blend about 3 minutes. # 26, # 34
4. Heat the remaining butter, stir in the flour with a whisk. Gradually add the milk, stirring vigorously with the whisk. Cook, about 5 minutes. Remove from heat

and stir in cheddar cheese until melted. Add nutmeg, salt, pepper and cayenne to taste.

5. Spoon the macaroni into a baking dish (10x7x2 ½). Spoon the meat mixture over the macaroni and pour the cheese sauce over all. Sprinkle top with parmesan cheese.
6. Bake for 30 minutes. Put under broiler to glaze the top

HUNGARIAN BEEF STEW

INGREDIENTS:

2 lb. boneless sirloin
2 tbsp. vegetable oil
2 cups chopped onions
2 tsp. finely mince garlic
2 cups chopped sweet red and green peppers
1 tbsp. sweet, mild or hot paprika

T1 tsp. caraway seeds
Salt and pepper to taste
2 cups chopped fresh or canned tomatoes
Sour cream for serving

DIRECTIONS:

1. Trim the meat of all gristle and fat. Cut meat into ½ inch cubes
2. Heat oil in a large sauce pan or heavy casserole. Add the meat and cook, stir the meat until it starts to brown (may have 2 or more batches).
3. Add the onions, garlic and peppers. Cook about 5 minutes.
4. Add the paprika, caraway seeds, salt, pepper to taste. Stir
5. Add the tomatoes; cover and cook for about 45 minutes on medium or low heat. Stir often
6. Sour cream option for individual topping

VEAL SCALOPPINI WITH MUSTARD

INGREDIENTS:

to 10 slices scaloppini of veal
Salt and pepper to taste
2 tsp. Dijon or Dusseldorf mustard
1 tbsp. mustard seeds

82 tbsp. butter
2 cups fresh tomato sauce or can

Note additional seasoning may also be used to taste

DIRECTIONS:

1. Cooking Veal is very quick
2. Pound the scaloppini between wax paper to very thin (without holes)
3. Spread about ¼ tsp of mustard on one side; sprinkle with mustard seeds. Do this on both sides
4. Heat the butter in a skillet. When hot add veal pieces. Cook the veal over very high heat to brown lightly on one side, about 30 seconds. The veal will cook very quick. Turn and cook for about 30 seconds on the other side.
5. Warm tomato sauce in sauce pan and spoon onto plate. Place 2 or 3 pieces of veal neatly on the sauce.

ROASTED VEAL CHOP WITH MEDITERENEAN SALSA

INGREDIENTS:

12 oz. Veal Chop
1 ea. Red and green bell pepper diced
1 ea. Tomato diced fresh
2 ea. Garlic cloves, chopped
1 tsp. capers

1 tbsp. black olives, sliced
4 oz. Italian bread crumbs
1 tsp. oil or butter melted 1 tsp. herb de Province

DIRECTIONS:

1. Brush chop with oil or butter on both sides
2. Put Italian breadcrumbs on a plate and press the chop into crumbs firmly to coat; do both sides
3. Heat oven to 400*F place chop in oven ready pan. Bake about 30 minutes and turn to bake 20 minutes more or until internal temperature reaches 160*F. Let rest about 5 minutes.
4. Mix diced peppers, tomato, garlic, capers, black olives and herb de province to make salsa.

GULF RED SNAPPER ENPALLIOTE

INGREDIENTS:

1 ea. Red snapper filet
1 tsp. onion powder
1 tsp. garlic powder
1 tsp. black pepper ground
2 oz. cream sauce

1 ea. Zucchini, squash, carrot, celery stick (all julienned)
1 ea. Red onion sliced
2 oz. Sprigs of saffron

DIRECTIONS:

1. Cut a piece of parchment paper 15x15
2. Place red snapper skin side down in middle of parchment
3. Season with onion, garlic, black pepper.
4. Take julienned strips to measure 1 ½ cups mixed
5. Slice red onion in half and thinly slice to equal ¼ cup; place all vegetables on top fish.
6. Fold sides together and crimp to form an envelope.
7. Bake at 350* for about 30 to 40 min. or until parchment starts to brown
8. When browning starts, remove from oven and let sit for 10 minutes.
9. Add saffron to cream sauce and heat; stir to release yellow color.
10. Pour on fish after opening envelope.

VEAL CHOP STUFFED WITH SPINACH AND CHEESE

INGREDIENTS:

4 veal chops (about 1 ½ in. thick)
Salt and pepper to taste
3 tbsp. butter
¼ cup diced onion
½ tsp. minced garlic
¼ lb. leaf spinach, trimmed
¼ cup soft bread crumbs
½ cup grated parmesan cheese
1 egg beaten

2 tbsp. pine nuts
¼ cup flour
1 tbsp. vegetable oil
3 tbsp. chopped shallots
½ cup white wine
½ cup chicken broth
½ cup diced fresh or canned tomatoes

DIRECTIONS:

1. Preheat oven to 400*F, cut a pocket in each chop; season chops on both sides
2. Melt 1 tbsp. of butter in a sauce pan and add onion and garlic. Cook until wilted. Add spinach; cook until wilted.
3. Remove from heat, add breadcrumbs, half of the cheese, egg, and pine nuts. Stir to blend
4. Stuff the chops with mixture, equally; close with tooth picks. Flour both sides
5. Heat the oil and 1 tbsp. butter in large skillet and add the chops. Cook 3 to 4 minutes on each side, then lower heat and cook for 5 to 6 minutes longer, turning often.
6. Sprinkle chops with the rest of cheese; remove. Pour excess fat off; add remaining butter and shallots. Add the wine to deglaze pan and cook until reduce by half. Add broth, tomatoes, salt and pepper to taste. Cook for about 5 minutes longer.
7. Strain sauce in a sieve, mashing solids. Spoon over chops

HOMESTYLE BURGER BY CHANO

INGREDIENTS:

2 parts to 1 part
93% lean ground beef=2 parts
Chorizo ground sausage= 1 part
Steak seasoning

Options:

Diced onion, mixed into burger
Pepper jack cheese, Hablenero cheese
Divide meat according to percent needed

CREAMY CHICKEN NOODLE SOUP BY CHANO

INGREDIENTS:

2 ea. Chicken breast cut into cubes
2 qt. chicken broth
1 jar chicken powder (Wyler's)
1 tsp. paprika, 1 tsp. black pepper
Adjust seasoning to taste

½ stick butter
2 cans Cream of Chicken Soup with herbs
Homestyle noodles

DIRECTIONS:

1. In a large pot add cut chicken
2. Add the remaining ingredients except noodles
3. Cook on medium high heat, stirring occasionally
4. Cook until chicken is done. Then add noodles and simmer until soup is done and noodles are soft.

CHICKEN WITH COCONUT APPLES BY DEBBIE

INGREDIENTS:

1 ea. Apple diced (red)
2 tbsp. lemon juice
1 tbsp. coconut oil or spray
1 ea. Chicken breast, boneless, skinless
2-3 slices bacon

DIRECTIONS:

1. Cook apples in coconut oil or spray using a sauté pan
2. Pound chicken breast, thin between wax paper sheets
3. Place apple mixture in middle of breast and roll. Wrap chicken with bacon
4. Bake at 350*F for about 30 to 40 minutes or until bacon browns.
5. Let it rest and slice

This recipe was designed by her when she had a special diet that required no oil, or special season.

PARMESAN BAKED SALMON

INGREDIENTS:

¼ cup real mayonnaise
2 tbsp. 100% grated parmesan cheese
½ tsp. ground red pepper (cayenne)

4 salmon fillets, skin removed
2 tsp. lemon juice
10 ea. Ritz crackers, crushed (about ½ cup crumbs)

DIRECTIONS:

1. Preheat oven to 400*F; mix mayo, cheese and pepper until well blended and let set
2. Place salmon on foil lined shallow baking pan. Drizzle with lemon juice
3. Top with cheese mixture; spread to evenly cover salmon. Sprinkle with cracker crumbs, and pat down.
4. Bake 12 to 15 minutes or until salmon flakes easily with a fork

TOMATO AND SPINACH PASTA TOSS

INGREDIENTS:

2 cups penne pasta (7 oz.) uncooked
1 lb. Italian sausage (hot or mild Italian sausage, casing removed)
1 pkg. (6oz.) baby spinach leaves
1 can diced tomatoes with basil, garlic and oregano, undrained
1 cup shredded low moisture mozzarella cheese

2 tbsp. 100% grated parmesan cheese
1 cup red, yellow, green bell peppers sliced
1 cup sweet onions sliced
1 tsp. onion powder, garlic powder, black pepper

DIRECTIONS:

1. Cook pasta as directed on package
2. Cook onions, peppers, adding seasoning; then crumble meat in the same large skillet.
3. Cook through, stirring occasionally; drain
4. Add spinach, tomatoes and juice; cook 4 minutes or until spinach is wilted, stirring
5. Remove from heat and cover to keep warm
6. Drain pasta; place in large serving bowl, add meat mixture and cheese
7. Mix and toss to coat pasta well. Serve

SLOW COOKER TERIYAKI CHICKEN

INGREDIENTS:

2 ea. Leg quarters
¾ cup sugar
½ cup packed brown sugar
1 tsp. garlic powder
1 tsp. ground ginger

1 cup soy sauce
¾ cup water
¼ cup vegetable oil
¼ cup pineapple juice

DIRECTIONS:

1. In a large bowl mix all ingredients except chicken. Mix well
2. Cut leg quarters into pieces and trim excess fat. Place into a reclose able bag; pour mix over chicken. Marinate in refrigerator for at least two hours.
3. Place chicken in slow cooker and pour 1 cup of marinade over it.
4. Cook on high for about 5 to 6 hours.
5. The meat will be very tender.

Serve with rice or roasted vegetables

ITALIAN STYLE CHICKEN

(VERY SIMPLE TO MAKE)

INGREDIENTS:

2 ea. 6 oz. boneless chicken breast
1 can diced tomatoes with basil, oregano, garlic
1 sm. Can tomato paste
1 ea. Yellow sweet onion sliced
1 tsp. Italian seasoning

1 tsp. onion powder
1 tsp. garlic powder
1 tsp. black powder
1 tsp. basil dried
2 tbsp. vegetable oil or olive oil

DIRECTIONS:

1. Heat oil on medium high heat.
2. Season chicken on both sides. Cook until browned on both sides. Add onion while chicken is cooking. Allow onions to become transparent.
3. Add diced tomatoes; cover cook about 15 min.
4. Add tomato paste (1 tsp. at a time) until sauce thickens. Lower heat and simmer covered about 15 min. Stir sauce occasionally.

Note: Serve with egg noodles or any pasta

MEDITERRANEAN COD

INGREDIENTS:

2 cod filets 4 oz. ea.
¼ tsp. salt
¼ tsp pepper
1 can diced tomatoes
½ cup canned slice black olives
1 tbsp. capers, undrained

1 tbsp. olive oil
1 tbsp. chopped basil
1 tsp. chopped fine garlic
2 tbsp. grated parmesan cheese
T tsp. onion powder, garlic powder, black pepper

DIRECTIONS:

1. Preheat oven to 400*F
2. Season fish with onion powder, garlic powder, black pepper and salt to taste. Arrange in single layer in baking dish.
3. Combine tomatoes, olives, capers, olive oil, basil and garlic in a small bowl. Mix well; spoon tomato mixture over fish.
4. Bake 15 to 20 minutes or until fish flakes. Sprinkle with parmesan cheese.

CHILEAN SEA BASS

ADRIATIC-STYLE

INGREDIENTS:

6 oz. Sea Bass filet
6 oz. Fresh Spicy Red Pepper Pasta
¼ cup Roasted Red Pepper Vinaigrette
3 tbsp. red wine
1 cup sliced red, yellow, green pepper
1 small yellow onion sliced
½ tsp. thyme
2 tbsp. basil
1 tbsp. chopped fresh parsley
1 ea. Garlic, peeled and chopped
Salt and pepper to taste
1 tsp. onion powder, black pepper, garlic powder
2 tbsp. extra virgin olive oil

DIRECTIONS:

1. Place fish in plastic bag and pour vinaigrette over and close. Marinate for about 1 hour.
2. Heat oven to 380*f. Heat a medium skillet to medium heat, add oil.
3. Add peppers, onion and seasoning, cook until onions are translucent. Add red wine and simmer; 2 tbsp. of the vinaigrette.
4. Place fish on a baking dish and bake for about 12-15 minutes until fish flakes

easily with a fork. Reserve marinate.
5. Cook pasta according to directions. Reserve some of the cooking liquid for sauce. Add cooked pasta, remaining marinade, and cooking liquid to pan with onions and peppers; simmer for 5 minutes.
6. Serve with fish and pasta.

Special Note: Fresh Pasta available at Nicole-Taylor's Pasta and Market

1134 E. 54th Street Studio C

Indianapolis, IN 46220

FRITTATA WITH BACON, RICOTTA AND GREENS

INGREDIENTS

12 oz. smoked bacon cut into ½ in. pieces:
1 cup sliced shallots or red onion diced small
12 cups assorted coarsely chopped green
(kale, chard, mustard greens and spinach

12 large eggs
½ tsp. kosher salt
1 cup freshly grated parmesan cheese, divided
12 oz. fresh whole-milk ricotta cheese (2 cups)

DIRECTIONS:

1. Preheat oven to 350*F; cook bacon in 12 in. oven proof nonstick skillet until crisp. Using a slotted spoon, transfer bacon to paper towel to drain
2. Pour bacon drippings into a bowl; reserve. Return 2 tbsp. drippings to skillet. Add shallots and sauté over medium heat about 4 min.
3. Add half of the greens and toss until beginning to wilt, about 1 min.; add remaining greens and sauté until wilted, tender and dry, about 15 min.
4. Transfer greens to plate; rinse and dry skillet. Beat eggs and salt in bowl add ¾ cup parmesan cheese, then greens and half of bacon. Stir in ricotta.
5. Heat 1 tbsp. of reserved drippings in skillet. pour in egg mixture; spread greens evenly. Sprinkle remaining bacon and ¼ cup parmesan over eggs. Cook until frittata is just set at edges, about 10 min.
6. Put pan in oven and bake until middle is set about 20 min.
7. Loosen sides and slide onto platter; let cool before cutting.

SWEET AND WHITE POTATO SPEARS

INGREDIENTS:

Note: rinse potatoes in cool water
3 ea. Sweet potatoes (1 lb.)
3 ea. Baking potatoes (1 lb.)
½ cup Zesty Italian reduced fat dressing
¼ cup 100% grated parmesan cheese
2 tbsp. chopped parsley-garnish

DIRECTIONS:

1. Preheat oven to 375*F
2. Cut potatoes into spears; toss with dressing
3. Place on lightly greased baking sheet
4. Bake 30 min. turn potatoes, sprinkle with cheese; bake an additional 30 min. sprinkle with cheese. Test for doneness

Garnish with parsley

BACON AND SPINACH PASTA TOSS

INGREDIENTS:

1 lb. wide egg noodles
1 cup Sundried Tomato Dressing
1-pint cherry tomatoes, halved
1 lb. boneless, skinless chicken breast chopped
1 bag (6oz.) fresh baby spinach leaves
1 cup shredded Italian Style Five Cheese Blend, divided
8 slices bacon, crisply cooked and crumbled
1 tbsp. olive oil

DIRECTIONS:

1. Cook noodles as directed. Drain, reserving ½ cup of the cooking water
2. Heat oil and dressing in a large skillet on medium heat.
3. Add chicken; cook and stir 10 to 15 minutes or until cooked through. Add tomatoes; cook 2 more minutes stirring
4. Stir in noodles and reserved ½ cup cooking liquid
5. Remove from heat; add spinach, ½ cup of the cheese and the bacon. Toss lightly to combine; sprinkle with remaining cheese.
6. Note: if spinach has not wilted, cover and stir for about 3 to 5 min. until wilted

PECAN CRUSTED HALIBUT WITH LEMON BEURRE BLANC

INGREDIENTS:

4 oz. pecans crushed
4 ea. 6oz. Halibut fillets
10 tbsp. chilled butter, divided (1 ¼ sticks)
½ cup chopped shallots or red onion finely chopped

¼ cup white wine
¾ cup whipping cream (heavy cream)
2 tsp. fresh lemon juice

DIRECTIONS:

SAUCE

Melt 2 tbsp. butter in a heavy medium skillet. Add shallots; sauté until soft, about 2 min. add wine and cook until most of the liquid evaporates, about 4 min.; then add cream and simmer until sauce thickens, whisking occasionally, about 4 min. Cut 4 tbsp. butter into ½ inch cubes. Add cold butter to sauce, a few cubes at a time, whisking until each is incorporated before adding more. Whisk in lemon juice and season with salt and pepper to taste. Remove from heat. Cover sauce to keep warm.

1. Crush pecans and place on a plate. Season fish with onion, garlic, black pepper.
2. Press filets onto crushed pecans to coat both sides.
3. Melt remaining 4 tbsp. butter in a large oven proof skillet; sauté until golden brown on bottom, about 34 minutes. Turn fillets over and transfer to oven and bake until fillets are just opaque in center, 7 minutes
4. Pre-heat oven to 350*F at the beginning
5. To serve, drizzle sauce over fish and garnish with lemon wedge or slices

SUN DRIED TOMATO GRILLED CHICKEN

INGREDIENTS:

½ cup Sundried Tomato Vinaigrette Dressing- divided
4 ea. Small boneless chicken breast halves or chicken thighs and legs
1 ea. Green and red bell pepper, cut into large strips

DIRECTIONS:

1. Preheat grill to medium high heat
2. Pour ¼ cup of the dressing over chicken and peppers in a reseal able bag; refrigerate 10 to 15 min.
3. Grill chicken and vegetables 12 to 15 min. or until chicken is cooked through (165*). Turning often and brushing with remaining dressing

BRUSCHETTA MINUTE STEAK

INGREDIENTS:

1 tbsp. oil
6 ea. thin boneless beef steaks (1/4 to ½ inch thick)
1 ½ can diced tomatoes with basil, garlic and oregano
1 cup shredded low moisture part skim Mozzarella cheese
1 tsp. onion powder, garlic powder, black pepper

DIRECTIONS:

1. Heat oil in large skillet on medium high heat
2. Add steaks with seasoning; cook 1 min. on each side or until very lightly browned on both sides
3. Pour tomatoes on top of steaks; add cheese.
4. Reduce heat to low; cover, simmer 3 to 5 min or until cheese is melted.

Note: Can use boneless chicken breast halves pounded to about ¼ to ½ in. thick

Cooking time may vary for chicken.

BRAZO CHICKEN SANDWICH- I.A.C.

INGREDIENTS:

1 ea. Boneless skinless chicken breast 4oz. to 5oz.
1 tsp. onion powder
1 tsp. garlic powder
1 tsp. black pepper

1 ea. Swiss cheese slice/ or Monterey Jack cheese
2 tbsp. tangy barbeque sauce (your favorite)
1 tbsp. butter

DIRECTIONS:

1. Heat skillet on medium high heat with butter
2. Season chicken breast; cook for about 5 to 7 min. on each side (test for doneness)
3. Lightly toast bun. Place cheese on chicken after your barbeque sauce
4. Create your sandwich your way

ESCARGOT ENCROUTE

INGREDIENTS:

6 ea. Escargot
Puff pastry sheet cut into 2 in. squares
1 tbsp. garlic butter (herbs-onion powder, garlic powder, black pepper)
1 tbsp. garlic cloves minced- mix with butter and seasoning

DIRECTIONS:

Put Escargot in garlic butter and wrap in puff pastry- add more garlic to taste

Preheat oven to 380*F

Put wrapped escargot on baking sheet and bake about 10 minutes or until pastry browns

Note: brush pastry with melted butter to add color

Make a sauce Beurre Blanc to place on plate then arrange escargot and garnish

CHICKEN MANDARIN WITH BANANAS

INGREDIENTS:

Chicken pieces, cut up-leg, thigh, breast
3 tbsp. melted butter
Salt and pepper to taste
½ tsp. ginger
1 tsp. onion powder, garlic powder, black pepper

½ cup almonds, sliced, toasted
½ tsp. paprika
½ cup parsley chopped
8 oz. mandarin oranges
4 ea. bananas, cut in to one inch pieces

BASTING SAUCE:

2 cups orange juice
½ cup dried currants
¼ cup mango chutney

½ tsp. cinnamon
½ tsp. curry powder
Dash of thyme leaves, dried

DIRECTIONS:

1. Arrange chicken in a buttered baking dish, brush with butter; season with onion, garlic and black pepper
2. Combine orange juice, currants, chutney and spices; cook in a sauce pan about 10 minutes, stirring to blend. Preheat oven to 350*F.
3. Pour marinade over chicken, and bake about 40 minutes. Baste often and test for doneness 165*F. Just before serving add drained mandarin oranges and bananas; heat quickly
4. Garnish with toasted almonds and chopped parsley.
5. Serve with rice or pasta

CHEESY BACON CHICKEN WITH MUSTARD SAUCE

MUSTARD MARINADE:

½ cup mustard (Grey Poupon)
½ cup honey
1 tsp. vegetable oil
½ tsp. lemon juice

INGREDIENTS:

4 ea. Boneless skinless chicken breast
1 tbsp. vegetable oil
1 tsp. onion powder, garlic powder, black pepper
8 ea. Slices bacon cooked
2 cups shredded Monterey Jack Cheese

DIRECTIONS:

1. Combine marinade ingredients, whisk to blend well
2. Place 8 pieces of bacon on a baking sheet lined with foil and bake for about 15 min. at 425*F until crisp; set aside
3. Put chicken in reseal able bag with 2/3 of marinade. Refrigerate for at least 2 hours.
4. Preheat oven 375*, season chicken.
5. Heat oven proof skillet with oil on medium high heat, cook chicken 4 min. per side until golden brown
6. Remove from heat, brush each piece with marinade. And stack 2 pieces of bacon on each piece.
7. Spread ½ cup of cheese on each piece
8. Bake skillet chicken 5-8 min. test for doneness 165*F
9. Serve remaining marinade on side

POMMERY TARRAGON SAUCE

INGREDIENTS:

1 cup capers
4 tbsp. fresh tarragon
1 ea. Yellow onion diced
2 tsp. salt
1 tsp. black pepper

¼ cup Pommery Mustard
¼ cup white wine
¼ cup white vinegar
1 cup olive oil

Combine in blender, hold for service

HAWIIAN COD BY LOIS

INGREDIENTS:

2ea. 6 to 8oz. Cod filets
½ cup pineapple crushed
½ cup tomato crushed
1 tsp. onion powder

1 tsp. garlic powder
1 tsp. black pepper
Salt to taste
2 tbsp. olive oil or vegetable oil

DIRECTIONS:

1. Heat oil in skillet on medium high heat. Season fish with onion, garlic, black pepper.
2. Sauté Cod in skillet on both sides until fish becomes firm about 8 min. each side, do not overcook.
3. Mix pineapple and tomato in a small bowl; when fish is almost cooked top pineapple mixture. Simmer about 2 min.

ASPARAGUS AND SCALLOPS

INGREDIENTS:

6 oz. fresh asparagus cut in half
4 ea. Jumbo sea Scallops
Dijon mustard
White wine
Angel hair pasta

1 tsp. onion powder, garlic powder, black pepper and salt to taste
2 tbsp. extra virgin olive oil
2 tbsp. grated parmesan cheese
1 oz. Kale fried or wilted

DIRECTIONS:

1. Heat oil in medium skillet to medium high heat.
2. Cook pasta according to directions and reserve
3. Sauté asparagus and scallops. Cook until scallops are opaque and asparagus is tender but firm
4. Deglaze pan with white wine; add Dijon mustard; stir until well blended.
5. Serve over pasta and garnish with kale.

RED SNAPPER WITH CUMIN CITRUS SAUCE

INGREDIENTS:

8-10 oz. Red Snapper filet
1 tsp. onion powder, garlic powder, black pepper and salt to taste
2 tsp. cumin
White Wine
4 oz. orange juice

2 oz. soy sauce
4 tbsp. flour
2 tbsp. olive oil or vegetable oil
Orange slices and orange zest

DIRECTIONS:

1. Heat oil in a large skillet to medium high heat.
2. Lightly flour fish and season with onion, garlic, black pepper on both sides.
3. Now brown on both sides about 5 to 8 min.
4. Remove fish to a warming platter and hold
5. Add wine to skillet with cumin, orange juice, soy sauce and orange zest. Cook stirring to create a sauce. Add fish back to skillet and cook about 5 minutes more.
6. Serve fish and spoon sauce over top. Garnish with orange slices.

THIN SLICED PORK WITH CRANBERRY RELISH

INGREDIENTS:

6 oz. Thin sliced pork medallions
2 tbsp. butter
2oz. Red wine (Pinot Noir)
2 tbsp. flour
3 oz. cranberry relish
1 tsp. onion powder, garlic powder, white pepper
Salt to taste

DIRECTIONS:

1. Heat butter in skillet on medium high heat
2. Flour pork and season with onion, garlic, white pepper
3. Sauté pork quickly on both sides until lightly browned. Add wine to skillet do deglaze the pan.
4. Stir to create a sauce.
5. Serve with cranberry relish slightly underneath.

SWORDFISH WITH CUCUMBER RED PEPPER A SCAPECE

(Pronounced ah Ske-pah-Chay)

INGREDIENTS:

1 medium cucumber, peeled, seeded and diced
Salt to taste
1 small onion diced
2 cloves garlic, minced
1 large red bell pepper, roasted, peeled, seeded and diced
Pinch cayenne pepper
Pinch cinnamon
1 tsp. sugar
4 tbsp. white wine
¼ cup Sundried Tomato Vinaigrette Dressing
2 tbsp. unsalted butter or extra virgin olive oil
4 ea.- 4 oz. Swordfish Steaks
1 tsp. onion powder, garlic powder, black pepper

DIRECTIONS:

1. Toss cucumber slices with ½ tsp. salt and let drain in a colander about 20 minutes. Season with onion powder, garlic powder, black pepper.

2. In a large frying pan, heat oil on medium high heat; add the onion and cook until starting to brown. Add garlic and cook 2 min. longer. Stir in cucumber slices and cook about 3 min. Stir in the roasted red pepper, cayenne, cinnamon, sugar, white wine, and salt to taste. Cook until the liquid has evaporated and the sugar starts to caramelize 3 to 5 min. Add the chopped mint leaves. Put into a bowl and reserve
3. Marinate swordfish in the Sundried Tomato dressing.
4. Same pan, add more butter. Season fish with onion, garlic, black pepper salt to taste
5. Cook until browned about 5 min. turn and cook about 4 min. longer.
6. Drain excess oil; put cucumber sauce back in pan to heat and absorb the swordfish cooking juices. Add remaining marinade to pan to heat.
7. Spoon the cucumber A' Scapece over the swordfish.

CUCUMBER AND SHRIMP SALAD

INGREDIENTS:

1 tsp. fresh lemon juice
Salt and fresh ground pepper to taste
2 tbsp. extra virgin olive oil

Salad:

1 large cucumber peeled, seeded and sliced thin
1 tbsp. white wine vinegar
1 tsp. sugar
Salt and pepper to taste
1 tbsp. olive oil
4 thin slices pancetta (unsmoked Italian bacon) chopped

1 lb. medium shrimp, peeled, and deveined, tails on
1 clove garlic, minced
1/3 cup chopped fresh basil
1 tbsp. capers, rinsed
Pinch cayenne pepper
Juice of ½ large lemon
1 bunch arugula rinsed

DIRECTIONS:

Dressing: Combine the lemon juice, salt, and pepper; whisk well until blended

1. In a bowl, toss the cucumber slices with vinegar, sugar and ½ tsp. salt. Let stand for 30 min. Then drain and pat dry.
2. In a large skillet heat the oil over medium high heat. Add the pancetta and cook until fat is rendered and started to brown 8-10 min. Increase heat, add the shrimp and garlic. Cook briefly until shrimp starts to turn pink, about 1 min.
3. Add the cucumber and sauté until the shrimp is cooked through, about 1 min. longer
4. Remove pan from heat; add basil, capers, cayenne and lemon juice. Taste; add salt pepper as needed
5. Toss the arugula with dressing and arrange on plates. Spoon the shrimp and cucumber on top.

ARUGULA OIL

INGREDIENTS:

Stems from Arugula and some leaves

Blanch stems in boiling water for 5 seconds to set the green color, then dunk them immediately in ice water to stop the cooking. Roughly chop the stems and put in a blender. Pour enough olive oil to cover them by an inch and blend until smooth.

Note: Color and flavor are great right out of blender. Can let oil steep for w4 hours in refrigerator and then strain out the pulp. Strained, it will keep up to ten days in the refrigerator

Good with beef or seafood

SWEET POTATO CAKES

INGREDIENTS:

2 lb. sweet potatoes, roasted, flesh scooped out
1/3 cup diced red bell pepper
1/3 cup fresh frozen or well drained canned kernels of corn
2 tbsp. minced parsley

¼ cup minced chives
1 tsp. salt
½ tsp. fresh ground black pepper
2 tbsp. olive oil

DIRECTIONS:

1. Cook the sweet potato flesh in a sauce pan over medium heat, stirring for 2-3 min. to reduce moisture. The potato should still feel tacky
2. In a bowl, combine the potatoes with the red pepper, corn, parsley, chives, salt and pepper to taste,
3. Using your hands, shape the mixture into 3 in. cakes about ½ in. thick
4. Heat ¼ inch of oil in a sauté pan until oil is very hot and reduce the heat to medium high
5. Slip in the cakes but do not crowd and cook until golden brown on both sides. Be careful not to burn

SPAGHETTI WITH ARUGULA, TOMATO, AND RICOTTA CHEESE

INGREDIENTS:

1 lb. dry spaghetti
½ cup extra virgin olive oil
Salt and pepper to taste
2 tsp. dried oregano

3 ea. Beefsteak tomatoes, cut into 8 to 10 wedges, ea.
6 oz. arugula washed, tough stems removed
5 oz. grated ricotta cheese

DIRECTIONS:

1. Cook the spaghetti in plenty of salted boiling water until al dente. Drain well, but do not rinse. While it is still hot, put in a large bowl and toss it with the oil, salt, pepper, oregano and tomatoes. Gently toss in the arugula. Divide and top with the grated ricotta cheese.
2. Serve immediately

ANGEL HAIR PASTA WITH TOMATO, AVOCADO

INGREDIENTS:

1 medium onion, sliced thin
3 cloves garlic, minced
3 tbsp. extra virgin olive oil
½ cup red wine
2 tbsp. coarsely chopped fresh oregano
½ cup coarsely chopped fresh parsley, basil, or cilantro or a combination
2 lb. tomatoes, peeled, seeded and chopped (save all juices)
2 tbsp. capers
1 habanero or other Chile pepper, cored, seeded and chopped fine
Salt and pepper to taste
1 lb. dried angel hair pasta (Capellini)
1 ea. Avocado, sliced
Grated aged Asiago cheese or parmesan cheese (garnish)

DIRECTIONS:

1. Heat a large pot of salted water to boil for pasta
2. Heat oil in a heavy pan, sauté the onions and garlic for 5 min. on medium heat. Add the wine and fresh herbs, bring to a simmer, cooking about 3-4 min.
3. Turn heat off; stir in the tomatoes, capers, and Chile pepper. Season with salt and pepper to taste.
4. Keep warm until pasta is done.
5. Cook pasta in boiling water until tender. Drain but do not rinse and toss with the tomato sauce. Garnish with avocado slices and grated cheese.

Note: Great side dish

COD WITH CAPERS AND ONIONS

INGREDIENTS:

4 ea. 6 oz. Cod fillets
Salt and pepper to taste
1 tsp. onion powder
1 tsp. garlic powder
1 tbsp. olive oil
6 tbsp. butter
2 large onions, sliced
1 cup white wine

¾ cup reduced sodium chicken stock
1 ea. Seedless cucumber, peeled and cut into slices or strips
2 tbsp. drained capers
1 tbsp. fresh parsley, chopped

DIRECTIONS:

1. Season fish with onion, garlic, and black pepper. Heat oil and 2 tbsp. of butter in a large sauté pan. Add fish; sauté on medium high heat until light brown, 3 min. on ea. Side
2. Remove fish with spatula and keep warm. Pour off most of the fat and add onions. Cook onions until they are soft and caramelized, about 8 min.
3. Add wine, stock and bring to a boil, scraping the bottom of pan until liquid is reduced by half and is syrupy.
4. Add fish back to pan; cook 1 min., basting fish with sauce.
5. Add the remaining 4 tbsp. of butter and shake pan until butter is blended into the sauce, (do not boil) and add the cucumbers, capers and parsley.
6. Serve with sauce spooned over the fish

SNOW CRAB LINGUINI

INGREDIENTS:

1 lb. Linguini dry
8 oz. Snow Crab meat/ imitation
1 cup tomato diced
8 oz. spinach fresh
2 tbsp. garlic minced
4 tbsp. white wine
4 oz. cream sauce/ heavy cream

1 tsp. onion powder, garlic powder, black pepper.
2 tbsp. shredded parmesan cheese
Salt to taste
2 tbsp. extra virgin olive oil

DIRECTIONS:

1. Heat oil in a large skillet on medium high heat. Add crabmeat and break it up, garlic, onion powder, garlic powder, black pepper and cook 8 to 10 min.
2. Add tomato, spinach; cook until spinach wilts. Add white wine, cream sauce, stirring to blend. Cook pasta per directions; drain. Serve with crab mixture on top. Garnish with parmesan cheese

ARUGULA AND ORANGE SALAD

INGREDIENTS:

½ tsp. dried green peppercorns
½ tsp. coriander seeds
3 ea. Navel oranges, peeled and cut into sections, juices reserved
2 bunches of arugula (enough to serve 4)
2 bulbs of endive, bottoms trimmed off, cut into ½ in. slices
1 tbsp. fruity olive oil
Kosher salt to taste
2 tbsp. good quality balsamic vinegar

DIRECTIONS:

1. In a spice grinder or a mortar and pestle, finely grind the peppercorns and coriander seeds together
2. Pass the spices through a fine sieve to remove any husk
3. Drain the orange sections (reserve the juices) and toss with the ground spices.
4. Toss the arugula, endive and olive oil and salt. In a small bowl, combine the vinegar and ½ tbsp. orange juice. Pour this onto the greens and toss again. Place greens on salad plate and top with oranges

CHOCOLATE CINNAMON SHERBET

INGREDIENTS:

½ cup plus 2 tbsp. unsweetened Dutch processed cocoa powder
1 cup sugar
1 tsp. ground cinnamon
Pinch of fresh ground pepper
Pinch of fresh grated nutmeg

1 cup water
1 can (12oz.) evaporated skim milk
1 tbsp. vanilla extract

DIRECTIONS:

1. In a small sauce pan, mix the cocoa powder, sugar, cinnamon, pepper, and nutmeg. Whisk in the water and bring to a boil, continuing to whisk to break up lumps and prevent burning
2. Turn down the heat and simmer for 2-3 min. until the sugar is completely dissolved
3. Remove from heat and add the milk and vanilla; let the mixture cool.
4. Put mixture in a glass bowl, then into freezer. When it starts to chill, stir at least once an hour until the texture looks like very soft ice cream. Freeze until it becomes firm like sherbet.
5. Serve in chilled bowls.

PERIGEAUX SAUCE

INGREDIENTS:

1 lb. fresh mushrooms, chopped
¼ cup shallots, diced
1 tbsp. black peppercorns
¼ cup butter

2 cups red wine (Pinot Noir)
1 qt. Demi- Glace or meat Glaze
¼ oz. Truffle peelings, chopped fine

DIRECTIONS:

1. Heat butter in a medium sauce pan on medium high heat. Add mushrooms, shallots, peppercorns; cook until mushrooms are soft
2. Deglaze pan with red wine, scraping pan to release all sediment. Add demi-glace and reduce liquid by half.
3. Strain and add truffle peelings. Hold for service

Note: Good with all meats, poultry and some fish

SWEET AND SOUR SAUCE

INGREDIENTS:

20 oz. pineapple chunks, can
1 tbsp. fresh grated ginger
1 ea. Green and red bell peppers, julienned
1 tbsp. soy sauce

1 tbsp. cornstarch
1 tbsp. white vinegar, distilled
1 tbsp. brown sugar

DIRECTIONS:

1. Drain pineapple juice into a sauce pan; mix soy sauce with cornstarch, mix all other ingredients ginger, vinegar, brown sugar and bring to a boil. Sauce will thicken, if not enough add more cornstarch and water (1-part ea.). Cook until sauce becomes clear. Add pineapple, peppers; cook about 10 minutes until peppers are done.
2. Reserve
3. Good over meatballs, chicken, pork, and Monkfish

MIXED SHELLFISH EN PAPILLOTE

INGREDIENTS:

Pinch of Saffron threads
¼ cup dry white wine
1 ½ lbs. assorted shellfish- choose three or four

1. Medium raw shrimp, peeled and deveined
2. Scallops, small or large (cut in half)
3. Clams or oysters, shucked
4. Crab meat

1 cup tomatoes, seeded and chopped
¼ cup chopped scallions (white part only)
Zest of one lemon
Salt and ground black pepper to taste
1 tsp. onion powder, garlic powder, Herb de Provence
Scallions

DIRECTIONS:

1. Crumble the saffron threads into the wine and let set in a warm place, until wine turns yellow
2. Heat the oven to 450*F
3. Divide the shellfish between four sheets of parchment paper (15x15)
4. Moisten with saffron wine and top with tomatoes, scallions, lemon zest and a little salt, pepper. Seal the package and bake on a sheet pan until puffy and browned, about 8 to 10 min.

Note:

One sheet of parchment paper folded in half, put ingredients on one side. Fold over and begin to crimp fold starting at one corner. Crimp and fold, continue this until you have a half moon shaped package.

Serve with rice, couscous or orzo pasta

SALT - SEARED SEA SCALLOPS

INGREDIENTS:

1 tbsp. kosher salt
1 lb. sea scallops, dried thoroughly on paper towels
Boiled Potatoes:
6 ea. New potatoes
2 bunches curly parsley washed, dried, stems removed
2 cloves garlic minced

2 hard boiled yolks
1 cup plus 1 tbsp. extra virgin olive oil
1 tbsp. red wine vinegar
¼ tsp. crushed red pepper flakes

DIRECTIONS:

1. Cut the potatoes in half and put in a sauce pan adding water to cover. Bring to a boil, lower heat to simmer and cook until tender, about 20 min. Remove from heat.

Green Sauce:

1. Combine parsley, garlic, egg yolks, 1 cup olive oil, vinegar, and red pepper flakes in a blender or food processor. Blend until smooth. Set aside

SCALLOPS:

1. Sprinkle the kosher salt evenly over the surface of 9 in. cast iron skillet and heat on high heat. Wait about 3 min., the salt begins to dance.
2. Gently place the scallops on the salt, leaving space around each one. Sear until small beads of moisture appear on the top of each scallop. With tongs, turn scallops over and place in skillet where the salt has not been disturbed. Sear until you see the sides become opaque 2 min.
3. Arrange Scallops around edge of plate, put potatoes in center and green sauce on edge of plate

Garnish with lemon wedge

SPANISH STYLE CHICKEN AND MUSHROOMS

INGREDIENTS:

2 tbsp. olive oil
4 ea. 5oz. chicken breast halves
2 cups sliced fresh mushrooms (8 oz.)
1 can tomato soup
1 tsp. oregano, basil, tarragon
Salt and pepper to taste
1 tsp. onion powder, garlic powder

½ cup water
2 tbsp. Burgundy or red wine (Pinot Noir)
Hot cooked Extra wide noodles per instructions
Fresh parsley
¼ cup sliced pimento-stuffed olives
1-2 tbsp. tomato paste for a thicker sauce- optional

DIRECTIONS:

1. Heat 10 in. skillet over medium high heat, using 1 tbsp. of oil
2. Season chicken with onion powder, garlic powder, black pepper and cook until brown on both sides. Remove chicken and set aside. Keep warm
3. Reduce heat to medium; add remaining 1 tbsp. oil and mushrooms. Cook until mushrooms are tender and liquid is evaporated, stirring.
4. Stir in soup, water, wine, oregano, basil, tarragon and stuffed olives. Heat to boiling and return chicken to skillet. Reduce heat and cover. Cook until chicken is done, 165*F, stirring often.
5. Serve with noodles on plate, then place chicken over it.
6. Garnish with parsley sprigs

PEPPER, ONION AND SMOKED SAUSAGE

INGREDIENTS:

1 lb. smoked sausage (beef, turkey, pork) skinless
1 ea. Green bell pepper, yellow, orange, red bell pepper
1 ea. Yellow onion sliced into strips
1 can Rotel diced tomatoes with green chilies
2 tbsp. vegetable oil
1 tsp. onion powder, garlic powder, black pepper
Long grain rice to serve 2

DIRECTIONS:

1. Cut sausage into coin shaped pieces
2. Heat oil in a skillet on medium high heat. Add onion, peppers with seasoning and cook until soft about 10 min.
3. Add can dice tomatoes; then add smoked sausage until heated through. Lower heat and simmer about 10 min. Stirring
4. Cook rice per instructions (we use rice in a boil-in-bag)
5. To serve place rice on plate and spoon mixture over top

CHILE BUTTER

INGREDIENTS:

1 stick unsalted butter
1 tbsp. Chile-garlic paste or Sriracha
2 ea. Anchovy fillets, minced
T1 tbsp. minced garlic
2 tsp. Chile flakes

¼ tsp. cayenne pepper
½ tsp. salt
1ea. Lemon zest

DIRECTIONS:

Cut the butter in 1 in. pieces into a bowl and set on the counter to soften. When it has softened, mix in all the ingredients, stirring to evenly incorporate them. Lay out some plastic wrap and spoon the mixture in the center. Wrap the plastic over and twist the ends to form a log shape. Refrigerate or freeze.

CHICKEN PIGNOLI

INGREDIENTS:

7 oz. Chicken breast, boneless, skinless
¼ cup Pinenuts
½ cup Red and Green seedless grapes
2 oz. Marsala Wine

2 oz. brown sauce
Flour seasoned with onion powder, garlic powder and black pepper
2 tbsp. oil or butter

DIRECTIONS:

1. Lightly flour chicken breast. Heat oil in a medium skillet. Add chicken; brown on both sides about 8 minutes each side.
2. Add Marsala wine to deglaze the pan; then add grapes and brown sauce.
3. Simmer about 15 minutes, sprinkle with Pinenuts on top.
4. Make sure chicken is done 165*F

SNAPPER A' LA VERACRUZ

INGREDIENTS:

¼ cup pitted and chopped green olives
2 tbsp. capers
1-pint cherry tomatoes
2 tbsp. fresh parsley or cilantro chopped
Juice of one lime
¼ cup extra virgin olive oil
Fresh or pickled Jalapenos, chopped

4 ea. 4-6 oz. Snapper filets (Cod, Halibut can be used)
1 tsp. onion powder, garlic powder, black pepper
Sheets of aluminum foil

DIRECTIONS:

1. Heat the grill to medium heat
2. In a mixing bowl, combine the olives, capers, cherry tomatoes, parsley or cilantro, lime juice, olive oil and jalapenos.
3. Fold four sheets of aluminum foil in half (14 in.). Season fish both sides; place skin side down parallel to crease.
4. Top ea. Fillet with ¼ of the salsa mix. Fold the foil over to cover fish completely; then roll the edges tightly to seal the package
5. Place packets on grill and close lid. Temperature inside grill around 400*F. Cook until done about 8 to 10 minutes.

Note: Fish should flake easily when pushed with aa fork.

PORK CHOPS WITH TOMATO GRAVY

(BY MAMA BROCK)

INGREDIENTS:

4 ea. Bone in pork shops (1 in. thick)
2 tbsp. bacon fat
2 tbsp. fine cornmeal (Anson Mills)
3 cups canned San Marzano tomatoes

1 tbsp. each kosher salt and finely cracked pepper
1 tsp. onion powder, garlic powder, black pepper

DIRECTIONS:

1. Salt the chops a lot and put in a reseal able bag. Refrigerate for at least 4 hours.
2. In a sauce pan, heat the bacon fat on high. Stir in the cornmeal with a wooden spoon. Reduce the heat to low stirring until cornmeal turns light brown, about 5 min.
3. Crush the tomatoes and add to pot. Raise heat to medium and simmer the gray. Stirring until it has thickened slightly about 10 min.
4. Heat the grill on high and remove the chops from the brine. Pat them dry and rub with oil and season.
5. Grill for 8 min. on each side for medium
6. Let rest and serve with gravy on top or side.

CATFISH WITH APPLE, BACON VINAIGRETTE

INGREDIENTS:

3 tbsp. Sherry vinegar
1 tbsp. Dijon mustard
2 ea. Shallots, minced
4 oz. bacon, chopped
¼ cup olive oil
8 large Swiss Chard leaves, chopped

1 ea. Granny Smith apple, sliced
Salt and pepper to taste
4 ea. Catfish fillets, 6 oz. each
2 tbsp. butter
Juice of 2 lemons

DIRECTIONS:

1. Whisk together the vinegar, Dijon, and 1 minced shallot
2. Heat a pan on medium and cook the bacon until crispy. Mix the bacon and drippings into the vinegar, along with 3 tbsp. olive oil
3. Heat a little oil in a nonstick skillet on medium. Add the chard and the other shallot; cook until chard wilts, about 5 min. Add the apple; season with salt. Move chard to a side plate.
4. Wipe out pan and add a little oil. Season the catfish and sear them until golden brown on both sides.
5. Remove them; add 1 tbsp. butter, ½ cup water, half the lemon juice to pan. Simmer until sauce thickens. Combine chard, vinaigrette, and sauce.
6. Pour over fish

Note: Rice is suggested to serve.

ULTIMATE GRILLED STEAK

INGREDIENTS:

½ cup steak sauce- your choice
½ cup Balsamic Vinaigrette Dressing
2 small cloves of garlic, minced
1 tsp. dried oregano leaves
2 medium beef rib eye steaks, about 8 oz. ea.

DIRECTIONS:

1. Mix the marinade, combine all the ingredients. Pour ¾ of the marinade over steaks in a reseal able bag. Save ¼ cup of marinade
2. Refrigerate 30 min. to marinate. Turn steaks to ensure even cooking
3. Preheat grill to medium high. Drain steak; discard marinade. Grill steak 4-5 min. on each side or until desired doneness
4. Let steak rest; cover with foil to keep warm and juicy.
5. Drizzle steak with reserved ¼ cup dressing mixture and serve

CRUSTLESS BACON AND CHEESE QUICHE

INGREDIENTS:

1 cup sliced green onions
1 cup chopped tomatoes
12 slices bacon
1 cup sliced fresh mushrooms

12 eggs
1/3 cup sour cream
1 cup shredded cheddar cheese
1 cup shredded mozzarella cheese

DIRECTIONS:

1. Heat oven to 325*F. Reserve 2 tbsp. onions and tomatoes. Cook bacon in large skillet until crisp. Remove bacon to a paper towel. Save 1 tbsp. bacon drippings and add mushrooms, cook and stir 2 min.
2. Remove from heat, chop bacon, add mushrooms with onions and tomatoes.
3. Beat eggs and sour cream until blended. Pour into greased 13x9 in. baking dish; top with bacon mixture and cheeses.
4. Bake 30 min. or until cent is set. Sprinkle with reserved onions and tomatoes. Let stand 5 min. before cutting

CHICKEN FETTUCCINE CACCIATORE

INGREDIENTS:

8 oz. fettuccine, uncooked
2 tsp. oil
1 lb. boneless skinless chicken breast, into bite size pieces.
1 cup ea. Green pepper strips and sliced mushrooms'1 can diced tomatoes, undrained
¼ cup Zesty Italian dressing
½ cup shredded mozzarella/ parmesan cheese blend
½ cup chopped fresh basil leaves

DIRECTIONS:

1. Cook pasta as directed on package
2. Heat oil in large nonstick skillet on medium high heat. Add chicken; cook and stir until no longer pink. Add peppers and mushrooms; cook 3 more min. stirring.
3. Stir in tomatoes and dressing. Reduce heat to medium low; simmer 5 min. or until chicken is cooked through.
4. Drain pasta. Toss with chicken mixture. Sprinkle with cheese and basil.

CHICKEN AND MUSHROOM DINNER

(FOIL PACK)

INGREDIENTS:

1 can condensed cream of mushroom soup
1 ¾ cups of water, divided
1 pkg. (6oz.) stove top stuffing mix for chicken
6 small boneless chicken breast halves
4 slices thin sliced smoked ham, chopped
1 ½ cups sliced fresh mushrooms
1 ½ cups frozen peas

DIRECTIONS:

1. Preheat oven to 400*F mix soup and ¼ cup of water. Combine stuffing mix and remaining 1 ½ cups water; spoon evenly onto center of each of six large sheets of heavy duty foil.
2. Top each with one chicken breast, cover evenly with ham, mushrooms, peas and soup mixture.
3. Bring up foil side. Double fold top and both ends to seal each packet. Leave room for het circulation
4. Place packets on a 15x10x1 in. baking pan.
5. Bake 30 to 35 min. or until chicken is cooked through. Remove packets from oven; let stand 5 min.
6. Serve by slitting foil

Note: Spray foil to prevent sticking

ALMOND CHICKEN DIJON

INGREDIENTS:

4 ea. Small boneless chicken breast halves
2 tbsp. light mayonnaise
2 tbsp. Grey Poupon Dijon Mustard
¼ cup slivered Almonds, coarsely chopped
1 sm. Yellow sweet onion sliced
1 tsp. onion powder, garlic powder, black pepper
4 tsp. Sundried Tomato Dressing –(EVOO)

DIRECTIONS;

1. Preheat oven to 375*F place chicken in lightly greased 13x9 in. baking dish
2. Mix mayonnaise and mustard until well blended. Spread top ide of each breast with 1 tbsp. of mayo mixture; sprinkle evenly with almonds.
3. Bake 20 to 25 minutes or until chicken is cooked through- 165*F
4. Place sliced onions on bottom of baking dish
5. Pour Sundried Tomato Dressing on top of onions
6. Place seasoned chicken breast with almonds on top of onion mixture
7. Bake for 25 to 35 minutes until chicken is cooked through 165*F

PRAIRIE LAND POT ROAST

INGREDIENTS:

1-boneless beef shoulder pot roast (2lb.)
½ tsp. salt
¼ tsp. pepper 1 tsp. onion powder, garlic powder, black pepper
1 bottle Catalina Dressing, divided
2 large onions, sliced

2 lb. Yukon Gold or all-purpose potatoes, peeled, cut into 2 in. pieces
1 lb. carrots, peeled, cut into 1 in. chunks
Water
2 tbsp. fresh parsley, chopped

DIRECTIONS:

1. Season both sides of roast with seasoning. Brown meat in a heavy large pot or Dutch oven on high heat in ¼ cup of the dressing. Turn to brown on all sides. Add onions; stir to brown.
2. Add remaining dressing, potatoes, carrots, and enough water to come about ¾ of the way up meat
3. Bring to a boil; cover. Reduce heat to low and simmer 2 hours or until meat and vegetables are tender.
4. Remove meat; slice thinly against the grain.
5. Sprinkle with parsley

SAUSAGE AND TOMATO RIGATONI

INGREDIENTS:

4 cups rigatoni pasta (8 oz.) uncooked
1 lb. Italian sausage, cut into chunks
1 ea. Red onion, sliced
¼ cup tomato paste

¼ cup Sun-Dried Tomato Dressing
¼ cup fresh parsley, shopped
¼ cup grated parmesan cheese

DIRECTIONS:

1. Cook pasta as directed on package
2. Brown sausage in a large non-stick skillet; drain. Stir in onions and tomato paste; cover. Cook 15 min. or until onions and sausage is done. Stirring add dressing.
3. Toss sausage mixture with pasta. Sprinkle with parsley and cheese.

PORK CHOP SKILLET WITH PEARS

INGREDIENTS:

4 ea. Bone in pork chops (1 ½ lbs.) ¾ in. thick
1 tsp. oil
¼ cup light Balsamic Vinaigrette Reduced Fat Dressing, divided
1 small onion, sliced
1 clove garlic, minced
1 tsp. dried rosemary leaves
1 can (15 ½ oz.) pear halves in juice, undrained
1 tsp. onion powder, garlic powder, black pepper

DIRECTIONS:

1. Heat oil in large non-stick skillet on medium heat 3 min.; season the chops and add to skillet brown on each side about 3 min. each. Remove from skillet
2. Add 2 tbsp. of the dressing, onions, garlic and rosemary to skillet. Cook about 3 min.
3. Return chops to skillet. Add pears and remaining dressing. Simmer on medium heat 10 min. or until chops are cooked through.
4. Spoon sauce and pears over chops

HALIBUT FLORENTINE

INGREDIENTS:

2 cups instant white rice, uncooked
2 cups warm water
4 ea. Skinless Halibut fillets
4 cups packed fresh baby spinach leaves
½ cup Sun-Dried Tomato Vinaigrette Dressing

1 tbsp. grated parmesan cheese
1 tsp. onion powder, garlic powder, black pepper
Foil sheets
1 sm. Sweet onion diced

DIRECTIONS:

1. Preheat grill to medium high heat. Spoon ½ cup rice onto center of each of four 18-inch-long pieces of heavy duty foil. Pour ½ cup warm water over each mound of rice; top with a fish fillet. Arrange spinach around fish
2. Spoon dressing evenly over fish and spinach. Bring foil sides up. Leave room for heat to circulate.
3. Grill about 10 min. Place a packet on a dinner plate. Cut slits in foil to release steam. Sprinkle with parmesan cheese
4. Option: use a skillet on medium heat; cook onions. Season fish. Sauté fish skin side up. Add spinach, cook until spinach wilts. Add ¼ cup white wine, ¼ cup Sundried Tomato Dressing, cover. Simmer about 10 min.
5. Cook rice as directed on package

CHICKEN FAJITAS BY MINDY

INGREDIENTS:

Juice from 2 limes
2 tbsp. olive oil
1 clove garlic minced
1 tsp. chili powder
T tsp. dry cumin

1 tsp. sea salt
1 ½ lbs. chicken strips
1 ea. Green bell pepper, sliced in strips
1 ea. Yellow onion sliced

DIRECTIONS:

1. Mix lime juice, garlic, chili powder, cumin, and sea salt. Add chicken strips (marinate over night) in a reseal able bag
2. Heat oil in skillet on medium high heat. Add peppers and onions; sauté until soft.
3. Add chicken strips; cook until done. Pour chicken marinade on; cook 3-5 min. longer

CREAMY CHOCOLATE PUDDING

INGREDIENTS:

2 ea. Ripe avocados, halved, seeded, peeled and cut up
¾ cup milk or soy milk
½ cup unsweetened cocoa powder
½ cup honey
2 tsp. gluten free vanilla

Directions:

In a blender combine all ingredients until smooth. Divide among dessert dishes.

Chill

SKILLET PORK CHOPS WITH BUTTER, BEANS, PEAS AND CHARRED GREEN ONIONS

INGREDIENTS:

4 ea. 6 oz. pork loin rib chops
2 tbsp. cut fresh Italian parsley
2 tbsp. cut fresh tarragon
2 tsp. shredded lemon peel
Salt and pepper to taste
1 tbsp. olive oil
6 ea. Green onions, cut into 2 in. pieces
1 15 oz. can gluten free butter beans, rinsed and drained
1 ea. 5 oz. package fresh baby spinach
1 cup frozen peas, thawed
1 tbsp. lemon juice
Lemon wedges for garnish

DIRECTIONS:

1. Preheat oven to 400*F, trim fat from chops. In a small bowl combine parsley, tarragon, lemon peel, salt and pepper. Sprinkle mixture over chops; rub it in with your fingers
2. In a large oven, ready skillet heat oil over medium high heat. Add chops to skillet; cook about 6 minutes or until browned turning once. Stir in green onions into skillet around chops. Transfer skillet to the oven. Roast for 10-12 min. or until chops reach 150*F. Remove chops and keep warm.
3. Stir in beans, spinach, peas and lemon juice with green onions. Cook until beans, peas are tender
4. Serve chops with vegetable mixture

CREOLE-STYLE SHRIMP

INGREDIENTS:

1 lb. fresh or frozen medium shrimp in shells
1 tbsp. olive oil
12 oz. fresh asparagus spears, trimmed and cut diagonally into 2 in. pieces
1 medium red sweet bell pepper, seeded and cut into ½ inch pieces
½ cup chopped onion
2 ea. Cloves garlic, minced

2 tbsp. gluten free all - purpose flour
2 tsp. Salt free-gluten free Creole seasoning
Salt and pepper to taste
¾ cup reduced sodium gluten-free chicken broth

DIRECTIONS:

1. Thaw shrimp, if frozen; peel and devein shrimp, leave tails. Rinse shrimp; pat dry
2. In a large skillet heat oil over medium heat. Add asparagus, sweet pepper, onion, and garlic; cook for 4-5 min. until vegetables are tender, stirring
3. Stir flour, creole seasoning, salt and pepper into vegetable mixture. Slowly stir in broth. Cook and stir over medium heat until thick and bubbly; reduce heat.
4. Stir in shrimp and cover, simmer for 1-4 min. or until shrimp are opaque. Stirring often

PARCHMENT BAKED HALIBUT WITH ASIAN VEGETABLES

INGREDIENTS:

4 ea. 6 oz. fresh or frozen halibut fillets
2 medium red, yellow sweet bell peppers seeded and cut into thin strips
6 bunches baby Bok choy, ends trimmed and leaves separated
¼ cup tamari or liquid Amino
1 tbsp. grated fresh ginger

2 tsp. rice vinegar
2 tsp. toasted sesame oil
¼ tsp. Asian chili sauce (Sriracha sauce)
½ cup thinly sliced green onions
2 tbsp. slivered tangerine peel (orange peel)
¼ tsp. freshly ground black pepper

DIRECTIONS:

1. Cut four 15 in. square pieces of parchment paper. Divide sweet peppers and Bok choy among paper sheets; top with fish.
2. For sauce, in a small bowl combine tamari, ginger, vinegar, sesame oil, chili sauce. Spoon over fish; with green onions, tangerine peel, and pepper
3. Bring up two opposite edges of paper and fold together several times to seal. Fold remaining ends to close, leaving space for steam to build
4. Bake for 15-20 minutes or until fish flakes. To serve open packets.

MEDITERRANEAN LENTILS

INGREDIENTS:

1 12 oz. jar quartered marinated artichoke hearts
1 16 oz. pkg. refrigerated steamed lentils
1 cup snipped fresh parsley
1 ½ cups thinly sliced and halved English cucumber pieces

1 cup grape or cherry tomatoes, halved
Salt and pepper to taste
½ cup crumbled feta cheese

DIRECTIONS:

1. Strain artichokes hearts over a small bowl, saving the liquid
2. In a large bowl stir together lentils and parsley. Add ¼ cup of the reserved artichoke liquid (enough to coat the lentils generously)
3. Stir in artichoke hearts, cucumber and tomatoes. Season to taste; spoon into bowl topping with feta cheese

CABBAGE AND CARROT SALAD WITH PEANUT SAUCE

INGREDIENTS:

1 4 oz. pkg. bean threads (cellophane noodles)
¼ cup gluten free chicken broth
3 tbsp. creamy peanut butter
2 tbsp. tamari or liquid amino
2 tbsp. honey
1 tsp. lime juice
½ tsp. toasted sesame oil
1 clove garlic, minced

3 cups shredded cabbage
1 cup shredded carrots
½ cup cut fresh cilantro
¼ cup chopped honey-roasted peanuts
Lime wedges for garnish
Note: Add grilled chicken (optional)

DIRECTIONS:

1. In a large bowl combine bean threads and enough hot water to cover; let stand 10 minutes. Drain well and cut into smaller strands
2. In a bowl combine broth, peanut butter, tamari, honey, lime juice, sesame oil, and garlic. Add cabbage and carrots; toss to coat.
3. Top bean threads with cabbage mixture and sprinkle with cilantro and peanuts. Garnish with lime wedges. Top with chicken optional

WINE BRAISED BRISKET WITH ONIONS

SLOW COOKER

INGREDIENTS:

1 3 to 4 lb. boneless beef brisket
½ tsp. kosher salt
½ tsp. freshly ground black pepper
1 14.5 oz. can gluten free beef broth
1 ½ cups red wine
10 oz. whole fresh mushrooms, quartered

2 large red onions, sliced
1 bay leaf
6 cloves garlic, minced
2 tbsp. cut fresh Italian parsley or chives
Salt and ground black pepper to taste

DIRECTIONS:

1. Trim fat from meat. Season with salt and pepper. Place into a 5-6 qt. slow cooker. Pour broth and wine over meat. Top with mushrooms, red onions, bay leaf, garlic and thyme. Cover; marinade in refrigerator for 12 to 24 hours.
2. Cover and cook on low heat setting 10 to 12 hours or high for 5 to 6 hours. Remove meat to a cutting board and slice
3. For sauce, transfer liquid to a large sauce pan. Skim fat from liquid; remove bay leaf. Bring liquid to boiling; reduce heat. Simmer, uncovered, until mixture reaches desired consistency. Season to taste
4. Serve sliced meat with sauce over it.

GREEK TURKEY BREAST (SLOW COOKER)

INGREDIENTS:

2 cups chopped onions red or yellow

½ cup chopped pitted Kalamata olives

½ cup snipped dried tomatoes, (not oil packed)

½ cup reduced sodium gluten-free chicken broth

2 tbsp. lemon juice

1 tbsp. gluten - free Greek seasoning blend

4 cloves garlic, minced

2 tbsp. olive oil

Salt and pepper to taste

1 ea. 2 lb. skinless, boneless turkey breast half

Crumbled feta cheese to taste

1 cup Greek yogurt

1 recipe Greek Cucumber Sauce

DIRECTIONS:

1. In a 4qt. slow cooker combine onions, olives, dried tomatoes, broth, lemon juice, 2 tsp. of the Greek seasoning, and the garlic
2. In a small bowl whisk together oil, salt, pepper and remaining 1 tsp. Greek seasoning. Brush turkey with oil mixture and put in cooker.
3. Cover and cook on low heat 6 hours. Remove turkey; slice. Put on serving platter, spoon mixture over turkey. Sprinkle with cheese

Greek Cucumber Sauce:

In a medium bowl combine 1 cup plain Greek yogurt, 2/3 cup peeled and finely shredded English cucumber, 2 tsp. fresh mint and 1 clove garlic, minced. Chill for 2 to 3 hours before serving. Serve on side

COD IN TOMATO SAUCE

INGREDIENTS:

4 6 oz. cod filets
1 medium lemon
1 clove garlic, crushed
1 tsp. red pepper flakes
5 tbsp. fresh parsley chopped
2-8oz. cans tomatoes crushed

½ tsp. sugar, ½ tsp. salt
2 tsp. oregano dried
1 tbsp. butte
1 tbsp. Olive oil
1 tsp. onion powder, garlic powder, black pepper

DIRECTIONS:

1. Season both sides of Cod with onion, garlic, and black pepper
2. Mix lemon juice, garlic, red pepper crushed tomatoes, sugar salt and oregano in a small sauce pan; heat over medium heat
3. Put Cod in a buttered baking dish, add lemon juice. Bake 30 min. at 350*F or until fish flakes.
4. Pour sauce over fish; garnish with parsley

APPLE-PISTACHIO CRISP

INGREDIENTS:

6 cups sliced, peeled cooking apples
3 to 4 tbsp. sugar
½ cup gluten free regular rolled oats
½ cup packed brown sugar
¼ cup gluten free all-purpose flour

¼ tsp. ground cinnamon
¼ cup butter
¼ cup roasted salted pistachio nuts, chopped

DIRECTIONS:

1. Preheat oven to 375*. Grease a 2-qt. square baking dish. In a large bowl combine apples and granulated sugar; spoon into baking dish.

2. Topping, in medium bowl combine oats, brown sugar, flour and cinnamon. Using a pastry blender, cut in butter until mixture resembles coarse crumbs. Stir in nuts. Sprinkle topping over apples.

3. Bake about 30 minutes or until apples are tender and golden brown. (do not over brown)

LOBSTER, CRABMEAT AND TORTELLINI

(ORIGINAL RECIPE)

INGREDIENTS:

4 oz. Lobster chunks
4 oz. Crabmeat chunks
1 small sweet onion diced small
2 ea. Mini Red sweet peppers, seeded, cut into coins
2 ea. Mini Yellow sweet peppers, seeded, cut into coins
2 ea. Mini Orange sweet peppers, seeded, cut into coins
1 tbsp. Extra virgin olive oil
1 tsp. onion powder, garlic powder, black pepper

10 oz. Tortellini mixed (spinach, egg)
¼ cup White wine (Pinot Grigio)
2 tbsp. Sundried Tomato Vinaigrette Dressing
2 tsp. garlic minced
Fresh Basil leaves for garnish

DIRECTIONS:

1. Cook tortellini according to package directions and set aside
2. In a large sauce pan, heat the olive oil; add the onions, mini pepper coins, the seasonings, onion, garlic, black pepper. Sauté until onions are clear. Then add lobster and crabmeat chunks breaking them up.
3. Add minced garlic and dressing.
4. Cook about 15 min. until lobster and crabmeat is hot. Add white wine and cover to simmer about 5 to 10 min. The liquid will begin to thicken. Add tortellini to heat through; toss to serve.

ABOUT THE AUTHOR

The author has created a guide to increase your knowledge about different types of food and how you might prepare it. The recipes in this edition have been tested in his own kitchen. Some of the recipes were modified for his wife and their unique taste and flavor profile. As he worked on this book, he realized that even though retired his love for cooking had grown. He began speaking to culinary students, within the DOC to pay it forward, the knowledge he had acquired. When you reach the age and time when memory is not at its best, he decided to write. This enabled him to create and possibly teach some of the things he has learned

He realized that a lot of students think it is easy to be a Chef. In retrospect, it takes lots of years of learning, refining, and practicing those skills you may have learned. A good school is essential in the transition. Learn everything you can to be the best that you can be.

You become a Chef when your peers acknowledge that you have achieved the title. He hopes you enjoy this edition and plans on many more in the future

www.ingramcontent.com/pod-product-compliance
Lightning Source LLC
Chambersburg PA
CBHW061125070526
44584CB00033B/4225